Men-at-Arms • 417

The Irish Defence Forces since 1922

Donal MacCarron • Illustrated by Bill Younghusband

Series editor Martin Windrow

First published in Great Britain in 2004 Osprey Publishing,
Midland House, West Way, Botley, Oxford OX2 0PH, UK
443 Park Avenue South, New York, NY 10016, USA
Email: info@ospreypublishing.com

CIP data for this publication is available from the British Library

ISBN 978 1 84176 742 0

Editor: Martin Windrow
Design: Alan Hamp
Index by Glyn Sutcliffe
Originated by The Electronic Page Company, Cwmbran, UK
Printed in China through World Print Ltd.
Typeset in Helvetica Neue and ITC New Baskerville

08 09 10 11 12 11 10 9 8 7 6 5 4 3 2

FOR A CATALOGUE OF ALL BOOKS PUBLISHED BY
OSPREY MILITARY AND AVIATION PLEASE CONTACT:

NORTH AMERICA
Osprey Direct, C/o Random House Distribution Center,
400 Hahn Road, Westminster, MD 21157, USA
E-mail: info@ospreydirect.com

ALL OTHER REGIONS
Osprey Direct UK, P.O. Box 140, Wellingborough,
Northants, NN8 2FA, UK
E-mail: info@ospreydirect.co.uk

www.ospreypublishing.com

Dedication

This book is dedicated to F.Glenn Thompson of Dublin, Vice
President of the Military History Society of Ireland, and currently in
charge of the uniform collection at Collins Barracks, Dublin. Glenn
is the leading authority on Irish military uniforms of all periods,
which he has researched and illustrated over many years; his other
interests include elite units in foreign armies.

Acknowledgements

I am greatly indebted to many serving and retired members of
the Defence Forces, including Capt. F.Costello; and to Glenn
Thompson, Simon Forty, James Perkins and Ruth Sheppard.
Special thanks are due to my wife, Monique, for her patience,
understanding and support.

Artist's Note

Readers may care to note that the original paintings from which
the colour plates in this book were prepared are available for
private sale. All reproduction copyright whatsoever is retained
by the Publishers. All enquiries should be addressed to:

Bill Younghusband,
Moorfield, Kilcolman West, Buttevant, Co. Cork, Eire

The Publishers regret that they can enter into no correspondence
upon this matter.

THE IRISH DEFENCE FORCES SINCE 1922

IN THE BEGINNING

THE GENESIS OF Irish Defence Forces uniform was that of the Irish Volunteers of 1913–22, formed to counter the Ulster Volunteers in the North, who were strongly opposed to Home Rule for all Ireland. This was promised by the then British Prime Minister, Herbert Asquith, but with the outbreak of the Great War it was put on hold. Members of the Irish Volunteers were encouraged to join the British forces (as were the Ulster Volunteers), and many thousands did, fighting bravely on the Western Front and elsewhere. Others, dedicated to an independent Irish Republic above all other considerations, declared this in arms during the Easter Rising of 1916. After the Rising the Volunteers remained in being, gaining strength and status from the general election of 1918 in which the Republicans gained an overwhelming majority. Their representatives stood on a platform of abstention from the British House of Commons, and campaigned for the establishment of an independent Irish parliament. The Volunteers, an autonomous body with its own Executive, gave allegiance to these representatives, who formed their own parliament – Dail Eireann – in 1919, when a guerrilla war against the British forces in Ireland slowly gathered momentum.

Two years of bitter struggle followed. The Irish forces involved were guerrillas or irregulars, flexibly organized, not usually uniformed or serving full time. Their organization was subject to differing factors of terrain and population; the pattern of operations was based on small groups of volunteers, not all of the same quality or degree of activity. The Flying Columns and Active Service Units were nevertheless structured into nominal brigades and divisions; and there were 16 of the latter by July 1921, when a truce was agreed. At this stage, the strength of the Irish Republican Army or the Volunteers was 114,652 officers and men. Statistical information is hard to come by, but on the Irish side 752 had been killed and 866 wounded; these included civilian casualties, but probably some 400 of the dead were combatants.

Many were deeply dissatisfied with the terms of the treaty which was negotiated following the truce; civil war was a possibility, as was social revolution, and perhaps even reoccupation by the British. The Anglo-Irish Treaty was signed on 6 December 1921, creating a separate state in six of the nine counties of Ulster which would still be

1922: A group of National Army men photographed at the barracks in Athlone Castle. Most have received the new caps, tunics, breeches and leggings, though some still wear civilian clothes; the tall officer at left foreground wears Irish Volunteer uniform with a slouch hat and what seems to be a leather coat.

governed from London, and the Provisional Government of the Irish Free State. This latter body then started to recruit a National Army on a regular basis from the ranks of the Irish Republican Army, and to take over the various barracks from the departing British forces. This new army, established by Michael Collins, was planned as a conventional land force supported by a small air arm, with a total strength of 4,000. The first appearance of the new force was the Dublin Guards, a composite unit of the IRA's Dublin Brigade, who wore entirely new uniforms and rank markings. Elsewhere troops wore Volunteer uniforms or, in many cases, civilian dress with military equipment.

The National Army

In February 1922 the Department of Defence under the new Provisional Government began to recruit volunteers for the regular army. General Collins picked men from the Active Service Unit of the IRA Dublin Bde and his own special 'Squad' as the nucleus. Properly uniformed and equipped, this unit marched past Collins at Dublin City Hall en route to take over barracks vacated by the British. About 3,500 men had enlisted by April 1922, but this figure was to multiply to 55,000 as a consequence of the impending civil war.

When the Dail approved the Treaty on 7 January 1922 the majority was only 64 to 57 votes, and dissension continued to brew. Many members of the IRA which Collins had led were dissatisfied with the terms of the Treaty, believing that they should fight on for a fully independent all-Ireland republic. In this atmosphere the new National Army was recruited from a revolutionary military organization, which had no sooner emerged from a successful guerrilla campaign with an external enemy than it was engaged in a bitter civil war. Its organization was not based on any military theory but rather on the basic principle of survival.

Initially the National Army loosely followed the order-of-battle of the War of Independence, but in October 1922 instructions to regularize enlistment, pay and organization were issued. A centralized system of reporting to GHQ was initiated, enabling the General Staff to plan their tactical operations in a way not previously possible – before this, local Army commanders had acted very much on their own initiative.

A dark green uniform was designed, based on that of the Irish Volunteers

1922: Armed, but not yet uniformed, a group of recruits for the National Army use a commercial vehicle. Not all would be raw novices, since a good proportion of recruits were IRA men who chose to follow Michael Collins.

and, apart from the colour and insignia, resembling contemporary British Army service dress. The peaked cap bore a bronze Army crest against a cloth diamond. The long-cut tunic had a stand collar, five large front buttons, two box-pleated patch breast pockets, two large side pockets, and shoulder straps sewn into the sleeve heads. Breeches or trousers were in the same colour and material as the tunic, the latter having turn-ups, and boots and leggings were brown. The officers' version was made up in a dark 'whipcord' material and the other ranks' in serge. These uniforms were to outlast the Civil War and would remain standard for 18 years, though with considerable styling and changes of insignia. The original unwired cap with its soft crown was pulled and pushed into some very unsightly shapes; the use of motoring goggles contributed to this, and personnel would parade in fairly well-cut tunics and breeches but with the effect marred by caps of all conceivable shapes.

Rank distinctions reflected the general styles of the Irish Volunteers' 1915 instructions, including cloth diamonds backing the cap badge (see Table A). Later, officers' ranks and insignia would be changed, but this original uniform was that worn by the nascent, and basically infantry Army in the Civil War. Supporting corps were developed in an ad hoc manner.

Table A: Rank distinctions, 1922

Rank	Cuff band	Cap diamond
Volunteer	none	none
Corporal	1 x green	green
Sergeant	2 x green	green
Sergeant-Major	3 x green	green
2nd Lieutenant	1 x blue	blue
1st Lieutenant	2 x blue	blue
Captain	3 x blue	blue
Vice Cdt (Bn)	2 x purple	purple
Commandant (Bn)	3 x purple	purple
Lt Cdt (Bde)	2 x brown	brown
Commandant (Bde)	3 x brown	brown
Lt Cdt (Div)	2 x red	red
Commandant (Div)	3 x red	red
Brigadier	1 x gold between 2 x brown	brown
Col Cdt	1 x gold between 2 x red	red

Collar & shoulder strap bars:

Cdt Gen (Div)	1 x gold between 2 x red	yellow
Cdt Gen (GHQ)	1 x gold	yellow
Maj Gen	2 x gold	yellow
General	3 x gold	yellow

Coloured staff stripes, worn along centre of shoulder straps:

Battalion	purple
Brigade	brown
Division	red

GHQ Staff cap diamonds, halved vertically:

Lieutenant & Captain	blue/yellow
Lt Cdt to Col Cdt	red/yellow

The Civil War, 1922–23

Each of the two sides into which the IRA split maintained that they were the 'true IRA'. Depending on their allegiances, the public at large labelled them the 'Free State Army' on the one hand and 'Republicans' or 'Irregulars' on the other. On 14 April 1922 the latter set up their headquarters in the Four Courts complex on the north bank of the Liffey in Dublin. Negotiations continued, but on 15 June supporters of the Treaty won a general election. The Irregulars disdained an ultimatum to surrender; and at 4am on the morning of 28 June the guns of the Army opened up from the south bank of the river.

The Civil War turned out to be an untidy one, without a clear-cut beginning or a definite end; in truth, neither side had prepared for a war. The artillery piece that was to breach the Four Courts stronghold was employed simply by looking down the barrel and opening fire. After hand-to-hand fighting the Irregular garrison threw their arms into the fires which had broken out, and surrendered. After the fall of the Four Courts the Army, using a single gun, armoured cars, mounted infantry and foot soldiers, captured the other Irregular strongholds in Dublin over eight days of confused street fighting.

On the day the war erupted, the anti-Treaty forces concentrated at Blessington in Co. Wicklow were preparing to move on Dublin when the Army launched a pre-emptive strike. Employing one of the first Bristol F2B Fighters from the new Irish Air Service, and artillery and armoured cars, the Army encircled the town; but the Irregulars escaped from this noose and dispersed south-eastwards into the hills.

The battle for Limerick city that followed was one of the war's major turning points. Victory there on 20 July opened the way for an Army sweep into the heart-lands of what the Irregulars called 'The Munster Republic'. Retreating, the Irregulars fought well-conducted rear-guard actions, making good use of covering machine gun fire while blowing bridges and felling trees as road blocks. However, on 2 August a landing at Fenit, Co Kerry, by the Dublin Guards, supported by armoured cars and artillery, threatened the flank of this 'Republic'. High explosive and shrapnel shoots over open sights at ranges up to 2,500 yards proved effective, and both flanks of the Irregulars' line were turned. Meanwhile, the Irregulars planned for a second time to isolate Dublin by severing lines of communication; this came to nothing when their battle plans were captured. The first phase of the war, in which the Irregulars attempted to maintain their hold upon towns and districts, was coming to an end.

Civil War, 1922–23: Lewis gunners front a squad of National Army troops, fully uniformed complete with greatcoats (see Plate A). Many wear disposable cotton 50-round bandoliers for .303in ammunition clips.

Whenever they retreated from their positions they used fire and explosives to hamper their advancing opponents: railway bridges were blown, the permanent way was lifted, stations destroyed, and roads cratered. There were still confrontations where considerable strength was employed, but the struggle had now degenerated into bitter guerrilla warfare, following the pattern of the earlier war against the British. Imaginative coastal landings led to the capture of Cork city on 11 August. The Army employed its 18-pdr guns and armoured cars with increasing effect; but despite its success in conventional operations, it suffered a grievous blow on 22 August when Gen Michael Collins was killed in an ambush in his native Co Cork. The nation and the Army mourned the passing, at the age of 31, of the outstanding personality of the generation that founded the modern Irish state. One thousand Irregular prisoners spontaneously knelt down and prayed for the lost leader.

A Command Training Depot was set up to give a hard three-week course in patrol duties, rounding-up operations, and the denial of the canals to Irregular boats. There were still ambushes on motorized troops, and both sides were responsible for outrages. To prevent the country from slipping into total anarchy, the government gave the Army increased power, including that of establishing military courts that could

1 September 1923: A major-general and two generals take the salute at a stand-down parade for a Civil War unit. On collar and shoulder straps the major-general displays one gold between two red bars; the generals, three gold bars. The central man still wears his cap badge on the old cloth diamond – for this rank, yellow.

Civil War, 1922–23: A National Army outpost guarding a railway siding – the railways were one of the Irregulars' priority targets throughout the war. The soldier in the foreground wears breeches and leggings with partial 1908 web equipment, the officer beyond him straight-cut slacks with turn-ups (cf Plate A2).

(and did) enforce the death sentence for those taken in arms. Shortly after the death of the Irregulars' chief-of-staff Liam Lynch in April 1923, his successor Frank Aiken ordered an end to offensive operations.

The anti-Treaty political leader Eamon de Valera published peace proposals, but the government would not budge from the principle that all political questions must be determined by the majority vote of the people's elected representatives (a principle de Valera had ignored when a majority of the Dail had voted in favour of the Treaty). De Valera issued a general order to cease fire and dump all arms on 24 May 1923. On that same day the last significant military action took place, when National Army troops captured the entire HQ staff of an anti-Treaty division, together with a huge store of arms, explosives and ammunition. The total killed on both sides came to approximately 4,000 – several times the losses inflicted by the British Army in 1919–21; and though an uneasy peace reigned, the deep wounds of the Civil War would not be healed for many decades.

The National Army had never yet known what it was like to be a regular peacetime army. On 3 August 1923 the Defence Forces (Temporary Provisions) Act 1923 finally put it on a statutory footing.

The first reorganization

On 31 January 1923, at the height of hostilities, a reorganization included an order for the 'Rearrangement of rank and insignia', as in Table B.

All officers were now recommissioned. The reorganization provided for only two types of staff officers: General Headquarters, and Command. To differentiate between them a new cap badge was authorized on 24 August 1923 – the standard Army crest, gilded and filled with coloured enamel; the grooves of the star were highlighted with red for GHQ and blue for Commands. The old cap diamonds lingered unofficially until prohibited in November 1923. Some devices to identify the wearer's Corps now appeared unofficially, and later elements of these designs were incorporated into the official badges first issued during 1924; officers with collar rank badges placed their Corps badges 'behind' these.

The demobilization of the Civil War army started in the autumn of 1923, and in February 1924 a memorandum set out the planned evolution into a new establishment. These reforms were reflected in the uniforms – with the onset of peace there was now time to attend to style and appearance. The uniform would remain the 1922 pattern, but with improvements, particularly to rank insignia, caps, collar badges, staff distinctions and orders of dress. The new rank badge sequence was as Table C; after a short initial period the NCOs' insignia were worn on both upper sleeves. Sergeant-majors and battalion quartermaster-sergeants were rated as warrant officers, and wore Sam Browne belts like the officers.

Generals and colonels had black patent leather cap peaks. The general officers' cap badge was embroidered in gold wire on scarlet, with the employment of major-generals indicated by the colour of the voided centre of the badge: those at the Department of Defence had scarlet centres, and those in Commands had green. A colonel's cap badge was of gilded metal. Officers and men of the Military Police had scarlet cap bands and black leather peaks. All other officers had cloth-covered peaks, and all caps were to show a distinct improvement in smartness, with stiffened crowns.

Collar badges for Corps and Services were in silver for officers and, slightly larger, in brass for other ranks. Initially officers with staff appointments wore on either side of the collar three-point coloured cloth patches bearing gold stars, the patch colours being as for the rank badge backings (Table C). However, this enhancement was short-lived; in 1927 it was replaced with metal and enamel diamond shapes. These were edged with gold 'rope', and their enamel centres in the appropriate colours bore either a gold eight-point star or an Arabic numeral.

RETRENCHMENT

At the beginning of 1929 a government economy drive at a time of world financial recession led to a considerable reduction in the strength of the regular Army, whose official title was Permanent Defence Forces (PDF). In order to retain a body of trained personnel, five types of Reservists were

Table B: Rank insignia, 1923

Rank	Bars, left sleeve
Private	none
Corporal	1 x green
Sergeant	2 x green
	Bars, shoulder straps
2nd Lt	1 x blue
1st Lt	2 x blue
Captain	3 x blue
Commandant	2 x red
	Bars, shoulder straps & collar
Colonel	3 x red
Maj Gen	1 x gold between 2 x red
Lt Gen	2 x gold
General	3 x gold

Table C: Rank insignia, 1924

Rank	Upper sleeves, red
Corporal	1 x bar
Sergeant	2 x bars
Coy QM Sgt	2 x bars below QM badge*
Company Sgt	2 x bars below Army crest
Bn QM Sgt	3 x bars below QM badge
Sergeant-major	3 x bars below Army crest
	Shoulder straps, bronze
2nd Lieutenant	1 x bar
Lieutenant	2 x bars
Captain	3 x bars
Commandant	1 x diamond + 1 x bar
Major	2 x diamonds + 1 x bar
Colonel	3 x diamonds
	Shoulder straps, embroidered gold on red:
Maj General	1 x diamond + 1 x bar
Lt General	2 x diamonds + 1 x bar
General	3 x diamonds

(* For QM badge, see Plate G3 detail)

Subaltern & field officers' bronze bars and diamonds, bearing interwoven Celtic designs, were mounted on coloured backings: GHQ scarlet; Command HQ blue; Bde HQ bottle green; Corps & Services lemon yellow; Infantry purple.

created: Reserve of Officers; Reservists Classes A & B; the Volunteer Reserve; and the Officers' Training Corps. The Infantry Arm formed nine Reserve battalions in 1929; these remained until 1935, and were composed of Reserve Officers with 'A' & 'B' Reservists. An A-type would have completed his regular service before transferring to the Reserve, while a B Reservist would have had three months' training before being placed on the Reserve.

The Volunteer Reserve had two units: the 1st (City of Dublin) VR Bn, and 1st (City of Cork) Field Battery. Uniforms and personal equipment for men of these two units were as for the Infantry Arm. The Dublin unit wore the standard Infantry badge underneath which, instead of numerals, the arms of the city appeared as a blue-enamelled shield, and blue cloth shoulder straps carried the title 'City of Dublin Volunteers' in brass. The Cork unit had plain blue shoulder straps.

The Officers' Training Corps was organized in five of the country's universities commencing in 1929. Detachments of two units were established at University College, Dublin, and a single unit at other academies. By 1932 total strength was approaching 600. The OTC uniform was that of the regular Army but with a 2in white cap band, brass collar badges of the appropriate institute, and detachable shoulder straps with brass titles in English or Gaelic. Trousers had white stripes, and the tunic had a green serge cloth belt with a brass buckle; when walking-out these young men wore a Sam Browne belt, and carried a cane with a nickel silver ball showing the Army crest. For social occasions a mess kit was worn, embellished with white shoulder straps with stripes of appropriate college colours.

In 1930 the Military College was established at the Curragh for regular cadets. Again a 2in white cap band was worn, bisected by a ½in green centre stripe. During training this was replaced with the other ranks' uniform. Officer's service uniform was worn for walking-out, and

An infantryman of the very late 1920s or 1930s operates a .303in Vickers medium machine gun. His M1928 helmet appears to be in the original dark green finish, but his 1908 webbing equipment is blackened.

Before mechanization, a mounted field artillery battery exercises; all ranks are in the 'battle order' of the 1930s. At right, an officer can be identified by his paler tunic and very pale cord breeches, and Sam Browne belt worn with both shoulder braces; at centre, the trumpeter's Grass sleeve badge shows up white.

the cadets' conspicuous cap band was often removed, in order to be less noticeable and perhaps to impress the girls.

The Air Service

The very first aircraft was a Martinsyde Type A Mk II biplane, purchased in 1921 from a war surplus company at Croydon, and held ready by two Irish ex-Great War RAF pilots (Russell and Sweeney) in case Michael Collins needed to escape from England if the treaty negotiations broke down. By the end of the year it had been joined at Baldonnel airfield by eight Bristol F2B Fighters, four Martinsyde F4 Buzzards, and four Avro 504 trainers, and early in 1923 by six DH9s and two more Avros. They were operated by the few score personnel of the new Air Service, and were active during the Civil War.

In 1924 the Service was retitled the Army Air Corps; two years later a cadet officer scheme was started, to build up a nucleus of trained pilots. In April 1928 the Corps' commander, Cdt James Fitzmaurice, was one of the crew of the Bremen monoplane which made the first successful east–west Atlantic crossing. Another six Bristols and two DH9s, four DH Cirrus Moths and one Fairey IIIF arrived before 1930. The 1930s were a time of neglect, when it was seriously suggested that the Corps be disbanded; nevertheless, a boy apprentice scheme for groundcrew began in 1936, and Aer Lingus began commercial operations from Baldonnel. On completion of their apprenticeship and Army commitments, these technicians went on to fill appointments with Aer Lingus or other airlines. The Corps acquired eight Vickers Vespas, and 18 newer Avro Tutor and Cadet trainers.

Peacetime soldiering

The ill-paid soldier of the 1930s could not afford to get away from barracks as often as he would have wished. Inspection parades were in any case regular and severe; and, with time on his hands, he lavished great care on his uniform, so that when he did manage to go out he cut a fine figure. At this time it was rare for a private soldier to get permission to wear civvies even when off duty, and in any event there was a lot of truth in a song current at the time: 'There's something about a soldier'.

When new boots were issued there was a dedicated procedure to be followed. First, the manufacturer's brown dye was scraped off until white leather appeared; then a good scrub with soap and boiling water eliminated all traces of oil and preservatives; next, a rub with fine sandpaper produced a short, fuzzy nap. Ten coats of red ink applied over a week gave the necessary scarlet base, onto which ruby-red polish was beaten and boned in with the back of a toothbrush, always kept moist with spit. The result was a mirror-like 'Chinese lacquer' finish. Some soldiers even flattened down the metal eyelets and polished them with Brasso. Not to be outdone, the infantryman treated his web equipment with a mixture of black boot polish and candle grease, which brought it to an almost patent-leather smoothness and brilliance.

Although the dark green serge uniform was extremely plain it had a certain sombre smartness; however, critics said that in the field the dark colour stood out prominently against nature's greens, and had no camouflage property. It was by no means a comfortable uniform: to encase the legs in tightly laced breeches and stiff leather leggings for the duration of a 20-mile route march or a 24-hour guard was a trying experience. The Irish Volunteers of 1913 had sported puttees, which every Great War army had found to be the most convenient legwear for troops; but when the new National Army uniform was being planned it was thought that by adopting leather leggings greater support would be given to the legs.

From 1926–28 a small sample batch of 'Adrian' steel helmets was tested; but they were not considered suitable, and in the latter year a heavier design was issued. Although the shells were made by Vickers Ltd, with the headband and fittings added in Dublin, the helmet was a direct copy of the German M1916 'coalscuttle'. The Army crest was attached to the front by welded-on metal loops. The helmets were originally painted dark green to match the uniform; but following wear-and-tear in the field they were invariably blackened, giving rise to the soubriquet 'The Black Uhlans'.

The Volunteer Force

When Fianna Fail (the political party formed in 1926 by the defeated Irregulars) came to Government in 1932, it was feared that it would take its revenge on its erstwhile Army opponents. This fear proved unfounded: in fact, matters improved a little for the emaciated regular force, particularly through the establishment in 1934 of a new reserve, the Volunteer Force, which also brought anti-Treaty supporters into the forces. While this placed a short-term training burden on the Army, the Volunteer Force would provide the nucleus for rapid expansion in the crisis of 1940. During the 1930s the regular Army had been allowed to run down to a mere five infantry battalions, known collectively as the Regiment of Rifles, and was disastrously short of men and equipment – even allowing for the economic situation at the time.

This new reserve was to be organized into three 'Lines' or categories, which would furnish a number of complete units on the basis of territorial regiments. Initial training of

1939: Army motorcyclists of the Supply & Transport Service pay close attention to their instructor, Stanley Woods (right) – an internationally famous rider in the interwar years, who captured more Senior TT prizes on the Isle of Man than anyone else. Woods is seen here in the uniform of a second lieutenant of the Volunteer Force (cf Plate C1); he subsequently rose to the rank of major. His green-faced tunic should be piped violet; it is visibly paler than the soldiers' M1924 uniforms. Note the tall outline of the forage ('wedge') cap, with its full-height folded false peak at the front.

14 to 28 days was supplemented by local drills, weekend and annual camps. Recruitment commenced in March 1934, and the initial response was good – within a year the overall strength was 11,531, of which 10,000 were First Line. The scheme envisaged a force organized into regiments bearing the names of ancient Irish territories which had existed prior to the dissolution of the old Gaelic order in the 16th century; it was felt that this would engender territorial *esprit de corps.*

The new VF gave a dramatic shot in the arm to the Defence Forces in general. The Infantry Arm was renamed a Corps, and would now be organized into ten named regiments. Enthusiasm ensured that some volunteer units rivalled the regulars in professionalism. Each of the ten regiments was to have a regular depot; two battalions of regular Reservists; and four battalions of Volunteers. It was the first scheme to make provision for recruitment into virtually all arms of the Irish service.

From its formation until the crisis of 1940, the uniform of the Volunteer Force was distinctly different from that of the regular Army, and had a strikingly Continental look. The design was based on a uniform planned for members of Sir Roger Casement's proposed 'Irish Brigade', which was to have been recruited from Irish prisoners-of-war in Germany during the Great War (a futile hope indeed). The uniform comprised a forage cap, tunic, breeches or trousers with turn-ups, all in a greenish-grey serge of a colour resembling German field-grey. The tunic was extensively faced and piped with green, and the legwear had a ½in green stripe. Bandoliers, web equipment, boots and leggings were black, as was a belt with the Army crest on a white metal buckle plate; all buttons and Corps insignia were white metal. The Volunteer Force officer had a similarly faced tunic but in the same green whipcord as the regular officer, with the same cream-coloured twill breeches. The Regiment of Pearse, which absorbed the Universities' OTC, followed the same pattern except that maroon was used as the facing colour, and in the centre of the forage cap. The mounts to badges and rank insignia were orange.

Each regiment was to have had its own distinctive insignia; a series of designs were approved and some badges were actually produced, but they were never on general issue. White metal collar badges of the various Corps – mainly Infantry and Artillery – were produced and worn, slightly smaller than the regular patterns. For the Regiment of Pearse the crests of the various universities and colleges were shown against an orange background.

By early 1939 world conditions had changed dramatically, and with them Irish sentiment; of 7,000 other ranks on the strength on 1 March 1939, only 3,000 re-enlisted. Nevertheless, on mobilization later that year many had a change of

Late 1930s: new recruits to the Volunteer Force are introduced to the Vickers machine gun; their uniforms are noticeably smart and well fitted. This design of forage cap would be taken into use by the whole Emergency Army during the war years.

heart, and the Volunteers provided a percentage of partially trained officers and NCOs, together with 6,000 men. Without them the vast expansion of the Defence Forces in 1940 could hardly have been accomplished. The appearance in 1940 of a new uniform for both regulars and Volunteers helped to obliterate the distinction between them: now they, and the flood of new recruits, were indistinguishable in appearance.

The scheme had not been pursued with the vigour it required, although by 1938 it was obvious that a Continental war was inevitable. The plans of those working on a new War Organization had to be realistic and capable of quick implementation; and the dire economic situation meant that calling large numbers of men to the colours would have disrupted the productivity and administration of a small and impoverished nation. However, there was a faint echo of how the scheme might have worked in the names of many battalions which served throughout the war years.

Late 1930s: an ambassador presenting his credentials, flanked by two Irish honorary aides-de-camp wearing 1935 pattern officers' full dress uniform (see Plate D). The Air Corps officer at left wears the 'mounted' style, with plastron front, in that Corps' unique steel-blue colour; the Infantry officer at right background has the single-breasted 'unmounted' uniform in midnight-blue.

Style and splendour

The first move away from the 'all green look' of the regular Army was in 1926, when a smart blue-grey mess dress with black facings was introduced for officers. The cap had a band of black 'shamrock' pattern braid; the shell jacket had black lapels, black edging and gold buttons, and the exposed waistcoat had small buttons. Staff officers wore on the lapels scarlet, blue or green gorget patches with a line of silver 'gimp'. Black-striped trousers were worn, with patent leather boots and nickel steel box spurs, and white gloves.

This uniform had a short life before it was replaced by an adaptation of green service dress: a tunic with detachable shoulder boards of yellow cloth, with rank insignia in silver wire embroidery (gold for generals), a cloth belt with a square gilt buckle, and trousers with a 1½in wide yellow stripe.

Starting in 1935, officers' full dress uniforms were introduced – first by the Cavalry, and gradually by other branches during 1936–37. In later years these have been denigrated as 'Ruritanian', but in fact they followed the basic pattern of the Belgian Army's contemporary design. Most features were common to all branches; the basic colour was black (midnight-blue), with differencing details in Corps and Service facing colours and 'metal'. Examples are illustrated on Plate D; see the plate commentary for a detailed description. These uniforms, purchased at individual expense, were not much seen after 1939, but remained regulation until 1955.

WORLD WAR II – 'THE EMERGENCY'

Sustained but frustrating efforts by the Army to improve its readiness were eventually rewarded by the placing of firm orders during 1939, but it was a case of too little, too late. Attempts to purchase equipment from Britain and later the USA met with little success; both countries were intent on trying to re-arm and re-equip their own neglected forces, and even firm orders could not be met.

At the outbreak of World War II – which was officially known in Ireland as 'the Emergency' – the Army mobilized in September 1939 at a strength of 19,136 all ranks (approximately 7,600 regulars, 7,200 Volunteers and 4,300 A and B Reservists). This figure represented not much more than half of the official wartime establishment of 37,560 men. Many units were never mobilized at all, and those that were averaged 30 per cent below strength. Yet between September 1939 and the crisis brought about by the fall of France in May 1940, Army strength actually decreased by nearly 6,000, due mainly to financial constraints.

At this crucial time in mid-1940 the Army was extremely ill-prepared to deal with such probabilities as a German invasion, or even a British incursion to repossess the Treaty ports and forts (those strategic enclaves which Britain had retained by agreement for some years after Irish independence). Belatedly, the parsimonious Department of Finance relented, and a recruiting campaign began in order to bring the Army up to a strength of 40,000 men. Due to an influx of recruits, the tasks of organizing new units combined with increased garrison and guard responsibilities left the regulars and the Volunteer Force just about able to organize mobile columns, of approximately company strength, for actual service in the field. These units comprised 11 Local Mobile Columns, each of rifle company strength; three Command Reserve Columns, two of which were of battalion strength and one a half-battalion; and one General Reserve Column of a single battalion.

It would take two years to develop these weak units into believable field formations, but the Army worked energetically to deliver an efficient – if inevitably rather lightly armed – fighting force. By the end of September 1940, approximately 30,000 new recruits were enlisted, mainly 'Durationists' or 'E-men' who joined up for the duration of the Emergency. Defence plans were drawn up, barracks and civilian accommodation were taken over, and intensive unit training began.

In the 1930s–40s the Army had only a handful of tanks, and these were used purely for training purposes, since wheeled AFVs were preferred for operations. These soldiers of the Cavalry Corps – note that corps' distinctive 'glengarry', foreground – are being instructed in the intricacies of a British Vickers Mk D medium tank.

In April 1940 orders were given for more practical uniforms and equipment for officers and other ranks. Changes to uniforms had been in the air in the immediate pre-war years; and a lighter green fabric ('bull's wool'), destined for a new tunic with a stand-and-fall collar, had been tested by being made up to the old design and issued to some units. Although referred to as 'battledress', the 1940 uniform still featured a four-pocket tunic; but the rankers' breeches and long leggings were replaced with straight trousers and short 'jam pot' gaiters. While this uniform was worn by all ranks for battle order, officers also had a service dress tunic with an open collar and lapels; rank insignia, buttons, etc., remained unchanged. Bucking the trend, the new recruits – and indeed some of the 'old sweats' – much preferred the old 1924 style standing-collar tunic, which was still being issued 'while stocks last'; they considered that this made for a more stylish or 'jildy' soldier, and youngsters would beg, borrow or steal to obtain the old outfit, which had a certain cachet. A forage cap (a tall sidecap, modelled on that of the pre-war Volunteer Force) replaced the old 'peaker'. Colonels received a new service cap with the generals' pattern cap badge and fernleaf peak embroidery.

New tricks were used to smarten up the 1940 uniform. Strings of lead weights were slipped inside the bottom of the trouser legs, so that the 'pull-downs' hung down sharply over the short gaiters; but the practice of stitching a permanent crease into the trousers attracted official disapproval. The forage cap fitted conveniently into a pocket, but at first everybody seemed to have their own 'angle' for wearing this headgear.

Initially, there were sufficient supplies of wool and leather to clothe the Emergency Army; but later in the war supplies of these commodities began to dwindle, and the tailors were kept busy trying to keep uniforms in reasonably serviceable condition.

NEW CORPS
The 'Saygulls'

The outbreak of world war led the Army to establish a number of new branches, one of them being the Coastwatching Service. Sites around the coast had been selected beforehand for Look-Out Posts (LOPs), and men who lived locally were enlisted into this special branch of the Volunteer Force to man them, since they knew their particular stretches of coastline intimately. Although unarmed, they represented the country's first line of defence – sentries who looked

1939: Infantrymen still wearing the M1924 uniform and M1928 helmet examine an imported British 5.5in Boyes anti-tank rifle, part of the trickle of supplies then being received. Britain was short of equipment herself, and was unwilling to part with much to an army which would be neutral in the looming war with Germany. Equally, it was in Britain's interests to help Ireland build up a realistic defence against German invasion, in order to safeguard Britain's western flank. Note, centre, a Cavalry Corps officer wearing the 'glengarry' – see commentary on Plate B3, page 43.

A Cavalry Corps scout rides off on his BSA20 at the head of his Motor Squadron; note the Irish-built Ford Mk V and VI armoured cars of the squadron's Armoured Troop in the background. The rider wears a glengarry, much distorted by his goggles; the standard greatcoat with Corps badges at the collar points, khaki canvas leggings, gauntlets, British 1937 pattern web equipment, and a slung SMLE rifle.

seaward for invaders, shipwrecked mariners of all countries, wrecked vessels, drifting sea mines, and encroaching aircraft. (One reason for their being unarmed was that in their lonely locations there was a danger that IRA elements – who were active during the Emergency – might attempt to seize weapons.) The coast watchers, who described themselves as 'Saygulls', lived at home, and their pay and conditions reflected this. They were given minimal military training, and though they were the butt of jokes by the troops, there was no fully trained soldier who could have got into the places on cliffs or slippery foreshores that they could. A total of 83 LOPs covered 2,800 miles of coastline, and if an incident occurred all the local watchers turned out, whether on or off duty. They saved the Ordnance Corps and Marine Service many wasted hours by accurately forecasting the movements of drifting mines, thanks to their intimate knowledge of the tides. They were highly competent in aircraft and naval recognition, and their preserved logbooks demonstrate their dedication as Ireland's 'radar'; as the war progressed their skill at recognizing aircraft types from the sound of their engines alone became formidable.

The usual post was built of concrete blocks with a large bay window looking out to the sea. Every post had a telephone – a not inconsiderable undertaking in the country at that time, and particularly difficult because of the remote locations. Communication was refined to a point where the coast watchers could report rapidly to a special section of G2 (Army Intelligence). After the fall of France aerial activity occupied more of their attention than sea movements. Each post had an open line to Air Defence Command which – much to the satisfaction of Britain – did not deliver just 'passive reports' but rather full plots of all aircraft over a period of time. The watchers were constantly on duty in shifts, reporting regularly to the control centre, including on-the-hour signals of zero activity. In the north-west, all RAF aircraft patrolling the Atlantic were logged, both outgoing and returning, and the Northern Ireland air bases often received information from the LOPs about the fate of their aircraft.

The Local Defence Force

At the time of the 'call to arms' in June 1940, the government asked those who could not join the regular forces to offer themselves for a new Local Security Force. As with the Emergency Army, in a couple of months that summer thousands of men both young and old joined up, and by October it was decided to separate the more active men into Group A and the remainder into Group B. Group A took men suitable for military service, and Group B those who would undertake auxiliary police duties. On 1 January 1941 the former became the Local Defence

Force (LDF), while the latter retained the original title of Local Security Force (LSF) and remained under the control of the police force – the Garda Siochana – wearing a slate-blue uniform.

The LDF eventually reached a total of 100,000 men, albeit with some natural wastage. Some early recruits did not stick the course, particularly when the invasion fears of 1940 diminished, and others could not continue for reasons of employment or domestic responsibility. However, their places were taken by young men in their late teens and early twenties, which dramatically lowered the average age of the force. Initially there were no uniforms, but within months a brown denim outfit was issued, consisting of a forage cap, blouse and trousers. Unlike the Lee Enfield rifles which were standard issue to the regulars, the LDF was armed with the .30in US Pattern 17, a slightly heavier and very accurate weapon. In addition to these, revolvers and various 'souvenirs' of earlier days appeared in the ranks; hand grenades were available, supplemented by huge numbers of home-made 'Molotov cocktails'.

A cap badge was issued (see Plate C), with the letters 'CA' for 'Cosantoir Aitiuil' flanking a harp. Before uniforms were available a brassard was worn with civilian clothing, in pale green with the letters 'CA' in black. Officers' insignia of rank were worn on the shoulder straps (see Table D).

From spring 1942 a green serge uniform, modelled on the British pattern 'battledress' and comprising beret, short blouse, trousers and overcoat, replaced the unpopular brown denim; British web equipment, haversacks and

Table D: LDF rank & appointment distinctions, 1940–45

Rank	Shoulder strap stripes
District Leader	2 x red, 1 x green
Asst Dist Ldr	1 x red, 1 x green
Dist Staff Officer	2 x green
Group Leader	3 x red
Asst Grp Ldr	2 x red
Grp Adjutant/Section Leader	1 x red
	Upper sleeve stripes
Asst Section Ldr	2 x red
Squad Leader	1 x red
From 1943:	*Shoulder strap stripes*
Area Engineer, Communications, Transport & Medical officers	2 x orange
Area Asst Adj & QM	1 x orange
District Leader (country), Executive Officer of Bn, Regt or Fld Ambulance (city)	3 x blue
Asst Dist Ldr (country); Training & Ops Officers, Adj, QM, Intel, Eng, Comms, Tspt or Med Officers of county or city Bn, Regt, Fld Amb; Coy, Bty or Sqn Leader	2 x blue
Assts to above ranks	1 x blue
	Left sleeve stripes
Coy, Bty, Sqn Adj or QM	3 x red
Asst Platoon Ldr	2 x red

Early examples of locally manufactured Ford armoured cars nearing completion; a former squadron commander praises the Fords for their reliability and robustness. Nevertheless, these Mk Vs were clearly so obsolete that they would have been doomed in any encounter with contemporary foreign equipment. The later Mk VI, which eventually equipped all the motor squadrons, was a superior vehicle; as late as the early 1960s a dozen of them gave sterling service in the Congo against the breakaway Katangan forces, which had some much newer Saladins.

groundsheets were also issued, and also – belatedly – bayonets for the P17 'Springfields'.

The bulk of the LDF was organized into rifle platoons and companies, which were consolidated in urban areas into battalions, and in the countryside into 'district groups'. Both had specialist engineer, communications and transport sections, and field ambulances. Some field artillery batteries were organized; and in Dublin all the cycling clubs came together into the 11th Cyclist Regt, subsequently the 11th Motor Regiment. The basic task of the LDF was to hamper and restrict an enemy until field forces could be deployed, by blocking and ambushing roads, blowing bridges, and cutting rail and telephone links; contact was to be maintained at all times and reported. Operating in their own familiar local terrain, the LDF was seen as the legitimate successor to the old IRA's Flying Columns. Like the Emergency Army, the LDF provided a common meeting ground for all citizens, regardless of politics, creed, class or calling, in the cause of national security and independence. Nowadays the LDF is often regarded as 'Dad's Army' or 'a bit of a joke', but the Chief-of-Staff held a much more positive view of these part-timers. At the end of the war the LDF became the FCA (the initials of the Gaelic name for its predecessor).

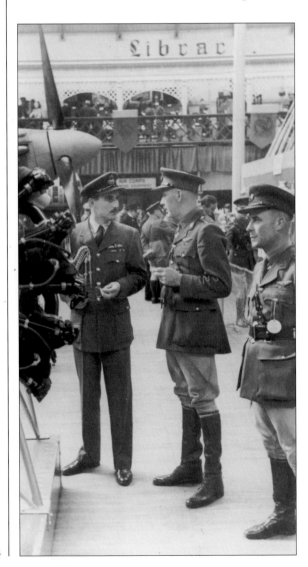

Despite Ireland's neutrality there was a good deal of quiet contact between the Army and their British opposite numbers, particularly between the Air Corps and the RAF. The British air attaché in Dublin is pictured (left), presumably discussing the Hawker Hurricane fighters which the Air Corps purchased during the mid-war years. The two Air Corps officers wear M1940 Army green and pale cord service dress, with the field boots which were an optional alternative to ankle boots and leggings.

The Construction Corps

This was a non-combatant element recruited from men aged 17–25 whose educational or physical standards did not meet basic Army requirements (when such standards were achieved it was possible for these young men to transfer to other Corps). The Construction Corps was employed on roadworks, drainage, turf-cutting (for the abundant fuel needed by both the military and the civil population), in forests and on general labouring, including improvements to aerodromes and ranges – and even, on occasion, on archaeological excavations. The Corps' five battalions wore Army uniform and insignia with a special collar badge. It was led by Army officers and senior NCOs, and during its short life it proved to be an interesting social experiment. The 1st Bn of the Corps was the first unit of the Defence Forces to have a shoulder flash: a red triangle with embroidered gold inscription and border.

The Chemical Defence Corps

This small unit of about 50 all ranks had a directorate, a chemical warfare company, a depot, a school and a laboratory. Its duties were to teach, supervise and organize anti-gas precautions throughout the Army. It also conducted research and experiments on war gases, training mixtures, and chemical media for detection and neutralization, coupled with the testing of anti-gas appliances, materials and clothing. Early in 1939 its functions were expanded into general Air Raid Precautions, to co-ordinate and supervise observation and early warning systems, shelters, communications and evacuation. Eventually it was decided that these operations could be handled more effectively by a branch of the General Staff in liaison with civilian authorities, and CDC personnel were absorbed into another headquarters branch.

The Marine Service

During the Civil War the new National Army had a small fleet of work boats which was – short-sightedly – disbanded thereafter. From 1924 until 1939 the Irish Free State (whose new constitution in 1937 changed its name to Eire) possessed no naval force. In accordance with the Anglo-Irish Treaty the Royal Navy patrolled the Irish coast, maintaining a base in Cork harbour until July 1938, while fisheries protection was carried out by the Department of Agriculture & Fisheries with the unarmed trawler *Miurichu* (lightly armed, and joined by the *Fort Rannoch*, in 1938). The belated formation of a Marine Service in 1939 brought six Vosper motor torpedo boats to join *Miurichu*, *Fort Rannoch* and assorted ancillary vessels. The disused RN dockyard on Haulbowline Island in Cork harbour was reactivated as the naval headquarters.

A conventional navy-blue 'square rig', very similar to the British patterns, was devised by the first director of the Service, Col A.T.Lawlor, for wear by the Marine Service and its reserve, the Maritime Inscription. The sailors' cap was surmounted by a blue 'bobbin' or pompon; cap tallies originally bore the ship's name but later simply 'EIRE', and hung down in ribbons behind. The blue jean collar, worn with a mid-blue 'silk' and dark blue (later, white) lanyard, had one broad outer and one narrow inner white stripe, and an anchor in each corner. Officers of the MS and MI were allowed to substitute cloth cuff rings, in maroon and green respectively, for scarce gold braid, and in some cases only the outer half of the cuff was covered. The Maritime Inscription wore black leather equipment from the Volunteer Force, whose uniforms had disappeared in 1940, with white gaiters when on parade. The original Marine officers wore a harp instead of the Defence Forces' cap badge; other ranks were issued with the Defence Forces badge in yellow thread on medium blue. The cuff rings (see Table E) were surmounted by an embroidered gold five-point star; Maritime Inscription officers wore a one-inch white cloth disc under the star, and other ranks wore this on the upper left sleeve. Specialist colours, between or below the cuff rings of officers and warrant officers, were purple (Engineer officers), medium blue (Administrative), and bottle-green (Technical). Rating stripes were worn on the upper right sleeve.

The Air Corps, 1939–45

The outbreak of World War II highlighted previous neglect, but 32 cadet pilots began training within the first year. A few more modern aircraft had been acquired. Four Avro Ansons

Table E: Marine Service rank distinctions, 1939	
Rank	*Sleeve stripes (gold)*
Leading Seaman	1 x (on jumper)
Petty Officer	2 x (on jumper)
Chief Petty Officer	3 x (on jacket)
	Gold cuff rings (on jacket)
Warrant Officer	1 x ¼ in
Ensign	1 x ½ in
Sub-Lieutenant	1 x ½ in + 1 x ¼ in
Lieutenant	2 x ½ in
Lieutenant-Commander	2 x ½ in, 1 x ¼ in between
Commander	3 x ½ in
Captain	4 x ½ in
Commodore	1 x 2in + 1 x ½ in

During the large-scale exercises of summer 1942, a company commander briefs his platoon leaders. Officers and men alike wore the M1940 uniform with battle order, and the officer at right displays Corps and formation insignia. His two shoulder strap bars identify a lieutenant; given the great shortage of trained officers during the Emergency, company commands often fell to sub-alterns. The shield-shaped Infantry Corps collar badge shows clearly, as do a formation patch (with a star motif) and a brigade bar on his sleeve. Note the chicken wire over the helmets, for attaching camouflage.

in 1937–39 were the Corps' first twin-engined, retractable-undercarriage type; and in 1938 four Gloster Gladiator biplane fighters were delivered, though Britain's own frantic rearmament put paid to a further order. 1939 brought three Supermarine Walrus flying boats, five more Ansons, and six Westland Lysander army co-operation aircraft. Ireland acquired 11 Hawker Hurricane Mk I and six Mk IIc fighters in 1943–45 (plus three force-landed RAF aircraft which were salvaged – as were a Lockheed Hudson and a Fairey Battle). Operational flights during the war were mostly coastal patrols by Ansons and Walruses from Rineanna; the fighters enjoyed shooting down drifting barrage balloons, but had no opportunity for aerial combat. Support types delivered during the war included 15 Miles Magisters, 13 Miles Masters, six Hawker Hind trainers and 13 Hawker Hectors. In 1943 sergeant pilots were trained for the first time.

When war broke out there was only one Army unit stationed in Southern Command, which covered Munster generally – a critical area for the defence of the country as a whole, on account of its airfields and harbours, its proximity to Europe and its position relative to trans-atlantic traffic. The two air bases on the Shannon – Rineanna (now Shannon International Airport), and Foynes flying-boat base – became increasingly important for the Allied cause. Military and civilian VIPs used both as vital transatlantic staging points. Despite Ireland's neutrality, even obvious warlike stores, urgently required in various theatres, were increasingly handled at these bases.

The safety of all this cargo, both human and material, as well as the facilities these bases offered an invader, required this area to be closely guarded, at first by one brigade, later reinforced by a second (7th & 8th Bdes – see 'Building Field Formations' below). These formations also guarded the whole Shannon Estuary, which was a vulnerable sea-lane into the heart of the country allowing the passage of heavy warships and troop transports 50 miles inland. The huge power station near Limerick, which provided power and light for almost the whole country, was also heavily guarded.

During the Emergency, technical personnel were involved in dismantling and rendering safe the 220 aircraft of the warring nations which force-landed or crashed in Eire, often in the most inaccessible parts of the country. Two, and sometimes three salvage teams were simultaneously involved, working in mountains, bogs, lakes and on the seashore to recover the remains of the various wrecks. Some aircraft were only slightly damaged, but even in the case of major crashes the engines, armament, and equipment represented valuable stock when returned to the RAF and USAAF across the Border in Northern Ireland; complete removal of the wrecks also saved unnecessary reporting by overflying aircraft. The disposal of ammunition, aerial torpedoes and bombs involved the Ordnance Corps: apart from public safety, such items could not be allowed to fall into the hands of 'dissident elements'.

Many incidents had an amusing aspect. When the US Army's LtGen Jacob Devers was returning to Washington via the UK after inspecting Mediterranean battlefields, his VIP B-17 Flying Fortress got lost and had to force-land in a field in Galway. Shortly afterwards a detachment from the 1st Infantry Bn surrounded the aircraft and took charge of its occupants and armament. As the Gaelic-speaking soldiers bustled about their business the general, clearly unfamiliar with the sound of Ireland's native tongue, was heard to remark, 'Gee, these guys sure know their codes'. This unit had been formed in 1924, almost exclusively from Irish-speakers from Connemara and the Aran Islands.

BUILDING FIELD FORMATIONS

Building 'all arms' field formations was a daunting task for a small Army suffering serious shortages of heavy weapons, equipment and staff officers. The small number of trained officers and NCOs faced many competing and simultaneous demands: immediate national security; providing trained cadres for new units – both of the combatant Corps and various specialist services – and raising and training them in their turn; organizing and leading the reserve organizations; and at the same time forming and practising field formations. Apart from the required new GHQ staff departments, training schools and courses of all kinds, and the core Infantry expansion, it was necessary to form: 2 x divisional staffs, 3 x brigade staffs; 1 x armoured, 3 x motor and 6 x cyclist squadrons, Cavalry Corps; 4 x field and 1 x 12-pdr batteries, Artillery Corps; 4 each x field companies of the Engineer, Signal, and Supply & Transport Corps, and the Military Police Service; 1 x field ambulance and 1 x hospital company, Medical Service; and a Civil Defence Firefighting Coy, Corps of Engineers.

Nevertheless, by 1942 great strides had been made. The early 'mobile columns' expanded into eight brigades; and six of these were further coalesced into two divisions. The 1st 'Thunderbolt' Division, commanded by MajGen M.J.Costello, had its HQ in Cork, and was charged with the defence of the vulnerable southern seaboard. Its main components were:

1st Brigade (HQ Clonmel): 10th, 13th & 21st Battalions
3rd Bde (HQ Cork): 4th, 19th & 31st Bns
7th Bde (HQ Limerick): 9th, 12th & 15th Bns

The 2nd 'Spearhead' Division, under MajGen Hugo McNeill, had its HQ at first in Dublin, and later at Maynooth; its mission was guarding the Northern Ireland Border, and its main components were:

2nd Bde (HQ Dublin): 2nd, 5th & 11th Bns
4th Bde (HQ Mullingar): 6th, 8th & 20th Bns
6th Bde (HQ Dublin): 7th, 18th & 22nd Bns

Each brigade also had a field regiment of Artillery, a Cavalry motor squadron, field companies of Engineers, Signals, Supply & Transport and Military Police, and a field ambulance.

The two independent brigades, and several other units which were not brigaded, functioned independently of the divisions as either Army Troops or Command Troops:

5th Bde (HQ Curragh): 3rd, 16th & 25th Bns
8th Bde (HQ Rineanna), partly formed: 1st & 23rd Bns
Garrison Bns: 14th (Dublin), 17th (Donegal) & 24th (Curragh)

The early deployment of the 7th Bde was in the Shannon area, including building a new and virtually impregnable coastal battery called Fort Shannon. By early 1942 all brigades were concentrating on building up equipment, training in combat efficiency, and erecting further defence works. At Rineanna more gun emplacements, blockhouses, tunnels and command posts were constructed, and defence of the air base passed to the latest formation, the 8th Bde (which became known as 'Rineanna Force'). Meanwhile, the 7th Bde continually rehearsed the defence of the port and flying-boat base at Foynes.

There was a long-held view that Ireland's strategic geographical position made an attack by Germany a constant danger, however unlikely that later came to seem; and even when the war was turning against the Reich a sudden diversionary swoop was not impossible. In summer 1942 the Axis was at its peak, with German armies advancing victoriously in North Africa and southern Russia, and Japan triumphant in the Pacific. That summer saw the largest series of military exercises ever undertaken in Ireland, devised by GHQ's Plans & Operations Branch to include various scenarios designed to test the troops to the limit. The long march of about 150 miles to the battlefield, and the return to bases – during which units were harassed by the LDF – became known as 'the Great Hike'. These 'war games' lasted for three weeks, and were realistic enough to cost several lives. The exercises were extensively covered by radio and the press, and the public (and interested parties overseas) were made aware that the

MajGen M.J.Costello (left), GOC of 1st Division, with members of his staff. The general wears the gold-on-red diamond and bar of his rank on his shoulder straps, and red gorget patches with a line of gold 'gimp'. Other officers display their bronze rank diamonds and bars on coloured cloth mounts, and (right) the small 'Thunderbolt' shoulder patch of 1st Division – see Plate F2.

troops had demonstrated an unprecedented level of professional skill-at-arms. Many useful lessons were learned, at all levels.

Many years later LtGen Costello, commander of the Blue Army in the 1942 exercises, observed:

'The strength that Britain or Germany would have had to deploy had they invaded went up rapidly from month to month. By 1941, our response to them would have been formidable, whereas, in 1939, troops could have landed anywhere in the south, for there would have been nothing to stop them. Had they landed in 1941, however, they would have needed an expeditionary force much larger than that which Germany used to conquer Norway. After Dunkirk, Montgomery [MajGen B.H.Montgomery, then GOC British 3rd Division] had been ordered to prepare his division to seize Cork Harbour. He rejected the task because he wanted two divisions and there was only one to spare. Of course, if all the British Expeditionary Force had got away from France, it is more than likely they would have made an attempt. For the Germans, the Shannon area and Foynes, with their air facilities, would have been more attractive targets than the southern ports.

'Had an invasion from either side taken place, a series of well-developed and documented counter-measures were in place. These included retreats to "centres of resistance" around certain cities and towns. It was reckoned that an invader could be held up for at least two months before these last-ditch measures would be needed and, thereafter, guerrilla tactics would make life uncomfortable and unprofitable for any invading force.'

Emergency heraldry

In 1942 those branches previously termed 'Services' were retitled Corps. In January 1944 the Adjutant General issued instructions which superseded all previous regulations, and confirmed all badges, insignia and devices brought into use by the immense expansion of the Defence Forces. Officers received new metal insignia with a raised centre for both bars and diamonds, both still bearing interlaced Celtic designs as before. There was a new distinction for a private 1st class: a red chevron on a green background, worn on the right cuff. Staff officers would now have plastic mounts to their metal insignia: General Headquarters, scarlet; divisional HQs, yellow; brigade HQs, green; and the staff at the Military College, orange. No mounts were authorized for other officers.

New collar badges were authorized: a bronze shield for the Infantry, with battalion numerals below; and the old pattern brass Artillery badge was miniaturized, being too long for the new uniform collar. The three companies of the Training Battalion were given an oval enamelled badge in red, blue or orange for the 1st, 2nd or 3rd Companies respectively. Other specialist badges which had been worn without authorization in pre-war days were now formalized: a drum or pipes for the Infantry bands, and crossed trumpets for

Table F: Formation signs, World War II period	
Formation	*Sign*
Army HQ Staff & DOD Coy	Green shamrock on scarlet shield
Army Troops	Green star on scarlet shield
1st Division	Curve-edged blue winged spearhead on orange shield
2nd Division	Straight-edged red spearhead on yellow shield
Eastern Command	Yellow star on rose-red shield
Curragh Command	Yellow star on pink shield
Southern Command	Yellow star on light green shield
Western Command	Yellow star on light blue shield
Military College	Green torch, yellow flames, on rose-red shield

Within each division or other command its brigades were identified by short coloured bars worn under the shoulder patch:

1st, 3rd & 7th Bdes	Green, white & orange respectively
2nd, 4th & 6th Bdes	Green, white & orange respectively
5th & 8th Indept Bdes	Green

buglers. Chaplains' tunic and greatcoat collar badges were placed on black cloth patches. Formation and Command signs, worn as small patches on the left shoulder, were retrospectively authorized (see Table F).

THE POST-WAR RUNDOWN

A post-war establishment calling for 12,500 all ranks involved rapid demobilization. What emerged was a regular Army composed of three brigades, one in each of the territorial Commands, each incorporating three infantry battalions and support units. In 1947 all reserve forces were disestablished, and replaced by the First Line Army Reserve and a Second Line Reserve entitled 'An Foprsa Cosanta Aitiuil' (FCA).

This organization continued until 1959, when the FCA was integrated with the regular Army. Six mixed brigades of regular and Reserve units were established, each with only one full-time regular battalion, with the intention that the remaining units would be filled by FCA personnel upon mobilization.

In 1946 revised rank insignia were also adopted, including the now-familiar 'winged' chevrons of flattened 'M' shape for NCOs, in red outlined with yellow (see Table G). In 1948 other ranks were authorized a new walking-out uniform with an open-collared tunic, but it was slow to reach the troops; there was much borrowing of this outfit from those who had it by those who did not when they were going out on a date. Post-war, the Command left shoulder patches increased in size. From 1950 a peaked cap once again replaced the wartime forage cap for both service and walking-out dress, but this was at first unwired and therefore rather unsightly. The old 1940 'bull's wool' tunic uniform soldiered on as service dress until 1961, after which it finally gave way to a new open-collared design in a smoother modern material, which is still worn today. At the same time the peaked cap was replaced for everyday wear with a black beret.

Poor pay, conditions and lack of equipment during the late 1940s and 1950s led to stagnation, but this changed with the onset of United Nations service overseas. The posting of observers to Lebanon in 1958, and a reinforced battalion to the Belgian Congo in 1960, highlighted the many shortcomings that had existed since 'the Emergency'. Pay and conditions now improved, and equipment was modernized; at the beginning of the 1960s the .303in Lee-Enfield was replaced with the 7.62mm FN self-loading rifle, and Panhard armoured cars replaced the Swedish Landverks and Irish-built Fords.

Since their earliest days the Defence Forces have marched to the skirl of pipes. This band wear 1946 uniforms (note the corporal's 'winged' chevrons): black glengarries with saffron bands and ribbons, and feather hackles; green cutaway tunics with extra 'doublet' buttons on cuffs and skirt pockets; saffron kilts; saffron cloaks with a large Celtic brooch on the left shoulder; yellow and green stockings with a tricolour diamond pattern round the yellow tops; red-brown shoes and belts. The pipes have dark green bags and cords with saffron streamers.

(continued on page 33)

THE 1920s
1: Corporal, Infantry, 1923
2: General Michael Collins, 1922
3: Private, Infantry, 1924

WRY. 04

A

THE 1930s
1: Major, Army Transport Corps, 1930
2: Sergeant, Artillery, 1936
3: Corporal, Cavalry, winter 1939

B

WRY. 04

THE 1930s–40s

1: Lieutenant, Artillery, Volunteer Force, 1934–40
2: Volunteer, Infantry, Volunteer Force, 1934–40
3: Volunteer, Local Defence Force, 1941

1

2

3

WRY. 04

C

OFFICERS' FULL DRESS, 1935–55
1: Captain, Infantry
2: Commandant, Signal Corps
3: Lieutenant, Air Corps

D

MOUNTED ESCORT, 1945
1: Trooper
2: Lieutenant

WRY. 04

'THE EMERGENCY', 1939–45
1: Corporal, 16th Infantry Bn,
   c.1942
2: Lieutenant, Infantry,
   1st Division, parade order, 1942
3: Gunner, Local Defence Force
   Artillery, c.1944

WRY. 04

F

UN CONTINGENTS, 1960–90
1: Corporal, 32nd Inf Bn; Congo, Aug 1960
2: Private, 25th Inf Group; Sinai, Nov 1973
3: CQMS, 68th Inf Bn; South Lebanon, Nov 1990

WR/. 04

G

HOME SERVICE SINCE 2000
1: Corporal, 5th Inf Bn, Permanent
   Defence Force, 2002
2: Private, Reserve Defence Force,
   2002
3: Trooper, 2nd Cav Sqn;
   Presidential Escort, 2003

H

By 1974 a whole suite of modern uniforms had been adopted: a green parka combat uniform and poncho, working dress with a reinforced woollen pullover, a light khaki overseas dress, and coloured fabric 'stable belts'. The most recent changes to combat dress, from 1999, are illustrated on Plate H.

In the early 1970s the situation in Northern Ireland emphasized the need for internal security rather than conventional defence, and purchase of equipment reflected this. The deployment of troops in the Border area highlighted the shortcomings of the 'FCA integration' policy, which was based on a conventional defence scenario. In 1979 a new organization separated the Permanent Defence Forces from the part-time FCA, and three new regular infantry battalions were raised specifically for Border security. In March 1980 the first female officer cadets were recruited, and female enlisted ranks the following year; previously only the Army Nursing Service had accepted women.

UNITED NATIONS SERVICE

The Republic of Ireland became a member of the United Nations in 1955. Three years later the Defence Forces provided unarmed observers for the Lebanon, their first UN mission. In 1960 the

After 1945 officers who possessed them still wore the dress uniforms of 1935–39; but in 1954 this less elaborate full dress in black barathea was introduced, and is still in use, though in a lighter weight than originally worn. The cap has the Army crest embroidered in gold on red, and gold chin cords. The shirt is white with a black necktie, or a bow tie for mess dress. The tunic has a cloth belt, gilt buckle and buttons, gold on red embroidered rank badges, and a gold cord lanyard. Collar badges are worn only by chaplains, whose trousers lack the red stripe.
Air Corps officers' mess dress is unique in being of conventional evening cut: a steel-blue shell jacket with gold buttons, cuff ranking, lanyard, and pin-on 'wings'; a white shirt, black tie, midnight-blue waistcoat and trousers. Following acceptance of female officer cadets in 1980, a black female mess dress was designed: a short jacket displaying the same rank badges and lanyard as the male tunic, worn over a square-necked dress with a long, slit skirt, both with gold lining (this is particularly striking when in motion).

Table G: Rank distinctions, 1946

Rank	Upper sleeves
Two-star private	2 x red stars
Three-star private	3 x stars in triangle
Corporal	2 x red winged chevrons
Sergeant	3 x winged chevrons
Coy QM Sgt	3 x winged chevrons below QM badge
Company Sgt	3 x winged chevrons below Army crest
	Shoulder straps & right cuff
Bn QM Sergeant	1 x red band on shoulder straps, red QM badge on cuff
Sergeant-major	2 x bands on shoulder straps, Army crest on cuff
	Shoulder straps
2nd Lieutenant	1 x diamond
Lieutenant	2 x diamonds
Captain	3 x diamonds
Commandant	crossed swords
Lt Colonel	1 x diamond + crossed swords
Colonel	2 x diamonds + crossed swords
Brig General	wreathed generals' badge
Maj Gen	1 x diamond + wreathed generals' badge
Lt Gen	2 x diamonds + wreathed generals' badge

Congo was the first mission to which Ireland contributed armed units in a potential combat role. The objective was to bring peace and order to a huge country that had until recently been a Belgian colony, but which had been granted independence at short notice, without a credible infrastructure to sustain it. UN contingents, notably those from Ireland and Sweden, attempted to provide some stability in a chaotic situation of rebellion, secession and tribal warfare. Despite the small size of the Defence Forces, Ireland contributed a series of six infantry battalions, two infantry groups and two armoured units during four years; a total of 6,191 Irish soldiers participated, of whom 26 lost their lives.

After the Yom Kippur War between Israel and Egypt, Ireland contributed a battalion to UNEF in the Sinai in 1973–74. The Northern Ireland crisis had a serious impact on the Army's international role, and between 1974 and 1978 large-scale UN commitments were abandoned because of domestic security needs. In 1978, however, the pattern of having one battalion serving abroad resumed, with Irish engagement in Lebanon. Following the Israeli incursion into southern Lebanon in March that year, the United Nations Interim Force in Lebanon (UNIFIL) was established to supervise the withdrawal of Israeli forces. When that was achieved the mission was reorganized and scaled down; but in June 1982 Israel launched a more wide-ranging invasion and occupation, making a partial withdrawal only in 1985. During 23 years the Defence Forces rotated an infantry battalion to Lebanon every six months, as well as providing approximately 100 personnel to UNIFIL headquarters and assisting the Mobile Reserve Force – a total of nearly 30,000 personnel. Throughout its lengthy stay the Irish battalion was headquartered at 'Camp Shamrock' near the village of Tibnin, from which it manned checkpoints and observation posts, patrolled extensively, and maintained a presence in many of the villages within its area of operations. It also provided humanitarian assistance in a variety of initiatives. The battalion lost 47 of its personnel before finally withdrawing at the end of 2001.

Since 1978 the Defence Forces have had a continuous presence on UN peace-keeping missions, and senior Defence Forces officers have been in overall command of several UN peace-keeping forces. The main missions to which Ireland has contributed include Cyprus, Costa Rica, Honduras, El Salvador, Guatemala, Nicaragua, Bosnia, Kosovo, Cambodia, Iran, Iraq, Afghanistan, Kuwait, Namibia, Western Sahara, Somalia, Tahiti and East Timor. Up to 1995 seven awards of the Military Medal for Gallantry had been made to members of these missions.

Originally, contingents were assembled from volunteers from throughout the Defence Forces; where possible, each of a battalion's three companies was formed from men of a single brigade. Later, each brigade was tasked with sending a company group overseas by rotation; some specialist personnel are attached from outside the parent brigade.

The new walking-out uniform with open collar, authorized for enlisted ranks in 1948, was of 'superfine' material of the same green shade as officers' uniforms. A great improvement over the old 1940 pattern, it was an inducement to prospective recruits, although slow to become generally available.

The extensive Irish participation in peace-keeping is regarded very positively both by the government and by the Defence Forces – so much so that in September 1993, when the government restated the roles of the Defence Forces, it defined one of them as: 'To participate in United Nations missions in the cause of international peace'. Ireland's peace-keeping role has promoted a positive image of the country and its Defence Forces within the international community, at the United Nations, and among all sides in mission areas. The late 1990s saw a change in the pattern of commitment, with Irish involvement in a number of UN-mandated missions controlled by regional alliances, including the NATO-led forces in Sarajevo and Kosovo, former Yugoslavia, and the Australian-led intervention in East Timor, as well as in military observer missions mounted by other regional blocs.

THE AIR CORPS and NAVAL SERVICE SINCE 1945

The Air Corps

Three Avro Mk XIXs replaced the Ansons in 1946; the following year the Hurricanes were replaced by 12 Supermarine Seafires (plus half-a-dozen Spitfire T9 trainers in 1951). A short service commission scheme from the late 1930s to the 1960s provided Aer Lingus with pilots, who retained Reserve commitments; 14 DH Chipmunk and ten Hunting Provost trainers were bought in the 1950s–60s. In 1956 the jet age arrived with three DH Vampire trainers, followed in 1961–63 by three more; this brought new concrete runways and other improvements to Baldonnel. The next major boost to morale came in 1963 with the formation of a search-&-rescue unit equipped with the first three of eight French SA Alouette III helicopters.

From 1972 eight Cessna 172 light spotter aircraft were acquired, for work along the Border. In 1975–76 six Fouga CM170 Super Magisters took over the jet training/light strike role, and equipped the Silver Swallows display team. In 1977 the first of 11 piston-engined SIAI-Marchetti SF260 Warriors were acquired for training, light attack and photo recce work. Maritime surveillance was shouldered from 1977 by two Beech King Air 200 turboprops, and since 1994 by two CASA CN235s with sophisticated surveillance and communications equipment. In 1986 the Helicopter Wing took delivery of five twin-engined SA Dauphin IIs. A small number of other general purpose types are now in service, and a squadron of Pilatus PC9M fighter-trainers has been added to the inventory.

For the last decade the Air Corps has been an independent Command of the Defence Forces, and in 1994 a blue uniform replaced Army green. The Corps is organized as a Headquarters; an Air Corps College; Nos.1 & 2 Operational Wings

27 July 1960: An officer and men of 32 Inf Bn, the first contingent formed for UN service in the former Belgian Congo, parade past the GPO on O'Connell Street in Dublin before flying out. They are dressed in the old M1940 uniform and 1937 pattern web equipment, and armed with Lee-Enfield No.4 rifles and Carl Gustav sub-machine guns. (United Nations)

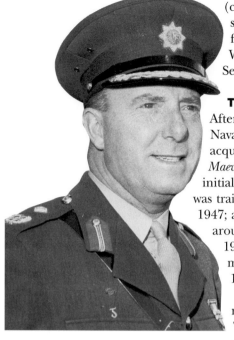

(comprising a training/light strike squadron, helicopter squadrons, a maritime squadron, a transport squadron and a fixed wing reconnaissance squadron); Nos.4 & 5 Support Wings (maintenance); and a Communication & Information Services Squadron. Current authorized strength is 930 all ranks.

The Naval Service

After the war the Marine Service was formally disbanded and the Naval Service was established in March 1946 as its successor. It acquired three wartime Flower class corvettes which were named *Maeve*, *Macha*, and *Cliona*. (These and subsequent ships bore the initials 'LE' for Long Eireannac, 'Irish Vessel'.) The first cadet intake was trained at the Britannia Royal Naval College, Dartmouth, UK, in 1947; and during the 1950s–60s the Naval Service had a strength of around 40 officers and 400 ratings. The corvettes were retired in 1968–70, and replaced in 1971 by three British-built coastal minesweepers – LE *Grainne*, *Banba* and *Fola* – which served until 1984–86.

In 1976 Irish territorial waters were extended from 12 miles to an Exclusive Economic Zone of 200 miles from shore. The need to safeguard sovereign interests in this greatly enlarged area increased the relative importance of the Naval Service, which grew to its largest ever size. In 1972 Ireland's first Irish purpose-built warship had been commissioned: built by Verlome Cork Dockyard, LE *Deidre*, an offshore patrol vessel of just over 1,000 tons, had a complement of 46 all ranks and armament of 1 x 40mm and 2 x 20mm cannon. She served as the class prototype for LE *Emer*, *Aoife* and *Aisling*, built between 1978 and 1980.

The helicopter patrol vessel LE *Eithne*, the NS flagship, was commissioned in 1984; displacing 1,760 tons, she has a complement of 85, mounts 1 x 57mm and 2 x 20mm cannon, and carries one of the SA Dauphin helicopters. The three minesweepers were replaced in 1988 by LE *Ciara* and *Orla*; these 712-ton coastal patrol vessels have a complement of 39 and mount 1 x 76mm cannon, 2 x 12.7mm HMG and 4 x 7.62mm GPMG. The Naval Service's newest ships are two larger offshore patrol vessels, LE *Róisin* and *Niamh*, commissioned in 1999

ABOVE **The Chief-of-Staff in 1961, LtGen S.McKeown, who took overall command of UN forces in the former Belgian Congo. Note the gold foliate edging to his leather cap peak; the staff gorget patches; the large wreathed sword-and-baton badge of general officers on his shoulder strap; and the small gilt cypher above his right pocket. This indicates that he is a Gaelic-speaker, and is the only civilian emblem permitted on uniform (apart from sprigs of shamrock on St Patrick's Day).**

RIGHT **Baldonnel, 1961: Men of 34 Bn – the third infantry contingent – board for the flight to the Congo. They still wear the old 'bull's wool' uniform with stiff service caps, though they have now received the FN rifle. Under magnification the elbow-length khaki brassard on the left arm, slotted to the base of the shoulder straps, can be seen to display 'IRELAND' embroidered in a large yellow arc above a green shamrock, above rank badges. Once in the Congo the blue and white UN patch was added between the shamrock and chevrons.**

2002: A three-star private serving with UNMEE, the UN mission to Eritrea. He wears the light blue UN beret with white and gold badge, and a matching scarf. The two-pocket summer combat shirt in DPM camouflage (see Plate H for colours) is cut long and worn outside the trousers. His name and rank respectively are displayed on a right chest tab, and a slide on the buttoning strap between the pockets. The national green/white/orange flash above his sleeve pocket is now standard on combat and working clothing. The green shamrock pin on his collar is non-regulation.

and 2001; displacing 1,500 tons, they have a complement of 44, mount the same armament as LE *Ciara*, and are capable of 23 knots.

The current seagoing fleet of seven or eight small to medium-sized patrol vessels have a respectable main armament and the capacity to interdict vessels in home waters and their approaches, launching boarding parties – whether benign or fully armed – as necessary. The Service also has an underwater search capability, operating portable side-scan sonar and an underwater remotely operated vessel (ROV); its diving teams include explosive ordnance disposal (EOD) personnel. The role of the Naval Service is best described as that of a 'constabulary navy', tasked with a range of duties of which the most important is fishery protection, but which include working in conjunction with the Garda Siochana, Customs & Excise, research agencies and other government departments. The Naval Service is divided into Operations Command, Logistical Support Command, and the Naval Service College. These structures maximize the number of sailors who are 'rotatable' to seagoing duty, which assists in the retention of trained personnel and provides a reasonable resource to underpin future operations. Current authorized strength is 1,144 all ranks. Under the Directorate of Reserve Defence Forces, the Naval Service Reserve is divided between the Eastern Group (Nos.1–3 Companies) and Southern Group (Nos.4 & 5 Companies).

At the moment the Service is not committed to Peace Support Operations, though it has obligations to train for these in order to support Army operations – since the Army has a definite commitment to PSO. There is a basic requirement for a Multi-Role Vessel (MRV) in the fleet; a great variety of 'capability suites' could be included in such a vessel, but a cost-conscious balance must be struck between essentials and 'nice to have' features. This is a delicate exercise, since such a vessel must be 'future-proofed' for at least 30 years ahead.

PRESENT STATUS

The Constitution of the Irish Republic vests supreme command of the Defence Forces in the President, a command which is regulated by law under the Defence Act (1954) and normally exercised by the government through the Minister for Defence. The Chief-of-Staff, who is appointed by the President, is directly responsible to the Minister for the performance of the duties delegated to him.

In 2003 the Army, Naval Service and Air Corps had an authorized strength of 10,500 personnel, male and female, plus some 250 in training, raised solely by voluntary enlistment. Its missions are to defend the state against armed aggression, to aid the civil power, and to participate in multi-national peace support, crisis management and humanitarian relief operations in support of the United Nations and under UN mandate, including regional security missions authorized by that body.

The Permanent Defence Force comprises three brigades, a Defence Forces Training Centre, a Logistics Base, and a number of special establishments. The brigades have geographical areas of responsibility: the major units of 1st (Southern) Bde are 3rd, 4th and 12th Inf Bns; of 2nd (Eastern) Bde, 2nd, 5th and 27th Bns; and of 4th (Western) Bde, 1st, 6th and 28th Battalions. Each PDF brigade has an authorized establishment of 2,330 all ranks, and is composed of:

Bde HQ
3 x Infantry Bns
1 x Field Artillery Regt, 1 x Cavalry Sqn,
1 x Field Engineer Company, 1 x C&IS Fld Coy,
1 x MP Fld Coy,
1 x Logistics Bn, 1 x Training Centre

The Defence Forces Training Centre, based at the Curragh, is primarily responsible for the military education of Defence Forces personnel; the Logistics Base, also at the Curragh, has a major stores function and also carries out repairs and maintenance on all types of military equipment. Special establishments colocated with the DFTC include the DFHQ C&IS Company and the Army Ranger Wing.

The Army comprises nine **Corps**: Infantry, Artillery, Cavalry, Engineers, Communications & Information Services, Medical, Military Police, Ordnance, and Transport & Vehicle Maintenance.

Infantry Corps The Infantry has nine Permanent and 18 Reserve battalions.

Artillery Corps The Artillery includes a directorate in Defence Forces Headquarters, and the Artillery School in the Defence Forces Training Centre. Field artillery units consist of three Permanent and five Reserve regiments, equipped with 105mm and 25-pounder guns and 120mm heavy mortars. The one air defence regiment, with headquarters in the DFTC, has four batteries: a regular battery in the DFTC and Reserve batteries in Cork, Limerick, and Dublin. Air defence is provided by the RBS70 missile system, and both L60 and L70 AD guns. Since 1962 the Artillery Corps has supported each Irish UN contingent with a heavy mortar troop.

Cavalry Corps The Cavalry's main function is to provide the primary reconnaissance resource of the infantry brigade. On UN missions it has contributed armoured car groups to the Congo and Cyprus and reconnaissance groups to Lebanon. The present establishment is six cavalry squadrons, three of which are Reserve, and one armoured cavalry squadron. It is mainly equipped with Panhard armoured cars and Scorpion tracked combat reconnaissance vehicles.

Corps of Engineers At the foundation of the state in 1922 a railway protection and maintenance corps was set up to repair damage inflicted during the War of Independence. In 1924 this was replaced by the

2003: Two Air Corps senior NCOs on parade during a 'wings' presentation ceremony, wearing the 1994 uniform in 'Air Corps blue'. The cap badge is embroidered in silver-grey on blue; it shows the eagle from the Corps collar badge, below a small 'FF' crest with a pale blue centre, above a spray of leaves. The rank badges on the forearm (see left) are in silver-grey braid with red details – see page 47. The white shirt is worn with a bright blue knit tie.

Engineer corps; and in 1931 field engineering companies and the School of Military Engineering were added.

Communications & Information Services Corps Formerly the Signal Corps, it developed from the communications organization of the Civil War, which had established a Headquarters Training School, Wireless Section and workshops in Portobello Barracks in 1922. Approximately 65 wireless stations were operated in barracks and posts during the Civil War. The Signal Corps was set up in 1924, grouping its school, stores and workshops in the Signals Depot, Curragh, during the 1930s. During World War II a field forces company, eight field, four garrison, Army Headquarters and Air Corps signal companies were operational. Today a field company is an integral component of an infantry brigade. The Corps has supplied communications for all units serving overseas on United Nations and European Union missions. The 1998 defence reorganization merged the Signal Corps and the Military Information Technology Section to form the present C&IS Corps.

Medical Corps Established in 1922 as the Army Medical Service, it comprises a directorate, the medical school of the Combat Service Support College, the Logistics Base Hospital (St Bricin's, Dublin), a medical detachment in the DFTC, and three Permanent and five Reserve field medical companies. Medical, dental, and pharmaceutical officers are commissioned as direct entries following professional qualification; enlisted personnel are trained in the medical school and with civilian institutions. Medical personnel have served with every overseas peace-keeping mission to which Ireland has contributed contingents.

Military Police Corps This Corps, formed in 1923, derives its authority from the Provost Marshal, who is appointed under the Defence Act (1954) 'for the prompt suppression of all offences'. A Military Police company is based in each brigade area, recognizable by the distinctive red beret. Personnel have regularly served in overseas peace-keeping contingents.

Ordnance Corps This Corps is responsible for the procurement and maintenance of all ordnance equipment and clothing throughout the Defence Forces, and for food and commercial catering services. It also provides the state's only bomb disposal (EOD) service.

Transport & Vehicle Maintenance Corps The Supply & Transport Corps, established on 2 May 1942, was re-established on 1 November 1998 as the Transport & Vehicle Maintenance Corps.

A number of other establishments include the following:

Army Ranger Wing This unit, directly answerable to the Chief-of-Staff and based at the Curragh, is trained to carry out specialist conventional and anti-terrorist operations. Conventional operations include operating behind enemy lines, securing vital objectives, and long-range patrolling. Anti-

1963: Col Kevin Curran, OC Air Corps, presenting aircrew wings to Flt Sgt Peter Sheeran of the Air Corps' new Helicopter Flight; both wear Army green uniforms of the 1961 regulations – the different qualities of material are evident. From 1961 the officers' breeches and long boots or leggings were superseded by straight trousers, and for all except parade order the Sam Browne was replaced with a fabric belt. The NCO wears the black general service beret introduced at about this date; his shoulder patch is the Air Corps' blue Command patch bearing the national colours as a Celtic boss enclosed by yellow wings. The badge of rank is as for company sergeant: the Army crest in red, over three 'winged' chevrons in red, outlined in yellow. All ranks wore the Air Corps collar badge.

terrorist operations include VIP protection, and handling aircraft hijackings and hostage situations.

Army Equitation School Established in 1926 and based in McKee Barracks, Dublin, its role has been to advertise and promote the Irish horse abroad and in Ireland. In 1928 the Russian instructor Col Paul Rodzianko introduced the classical training principles of Federico Caprilli. Since its inception the School has been the backbone of Irish show-jumping teams, and its riders have represented the country at Olympic, World and European championships. In the 1999/2001 season Army riders were members of the Irish team which won a record-breaking ten international team competitions (Nations Cups).

Reserve Defence Forces

The Permanent Defence Forces (PFD) are backed by the Reserve Defence Forces (RFD). With a total establishment of 13,500 (of whom 3,500 are female), the latter is composed of the First Line, a small number of time-expired regulars; and the Second Line, comprising a large number of part-time personnel, both military and naval. Not all units are up to establishment but the Reserves are now fully integrated and very active within the PFD.

The Directorate of Reserve Defence Forces is responsible for the *Army Reserve (under DFTC RDF HQ)* of 2x Inf Bns and 1 Field Artillery Regt; and for *1 (Southern), 3 (Eastern)* and *4 (Western) Bde RDF HQs*, each with between 4x and 6x Inf Bns, 1 or 2x Fld Arty Regts, 1 Cav Sqn, and companies of the supporting Corps.

* * *

The defence White Paper of 2002 – the first such document produced – envisaged a revamped Defence Forces with a clearer domestic role and a more focused approach to international service. The Defence Forces are to have a fully equipped infantry battalion in readiness at all times to participate in UN-mandated peace operations mounted by the EU Rapid Reaction Force. This poses a challenge, and demands a major effort in both unit training and re-equipment. This is being financed largely by the sale of surplus barracks and land, which should also lead to the greater concentration of forces and resources necessary for effective training.

The role of the Defence Forces remains a sensitive one in Irish political culture. The government has always taken the view that Ireland needs an army, primarily to counter

the internal security threat but also for symbolic ceremonial, and external purposes. There is a strong if vague attachment to 'traditional' military neutrality; but there has never been the political will to face up to the logic of that stance, which is to ensure that Ireland has the military means to act as a credible deterrent to aggression, as do other European states. Geography has ensured that Ireland has enjoyed the benefits of British and later of NATO protection; this has allowed the perpetuation of the illusion that a neutral state can protect itself from external aggression by fine words and declarations alone, and that neutrality equates with modest military needs. This attitude is changing slowly.

SELECT BIBLIOGRAPHY

J.P.Duggan, *A History of the Irish Army,* Gill & McMillan (Dublin 1960)

James J.Hogan, *Badges, Medals & Insignia (Irish Defence Forces)* (Dublin 1987)

Donal MacCarron, *Wings Over Ireland,* Midland Publications (Leicester 1996)

Donal MacCarron, *Step Together,* Irish Academic Press (Dublin 1999)

Karl Martin, *Irish Army Vehicles,* Cahill Printers Ltd (Dublin 2002)

G.White & B.O'Shea, *Irish Volunteer Soldier 1913–23,* Osprey Publishing, Warrior series 80 (Oxford 2003)

Periodicals:

An Cosantoir (Irish Defence Journal), published monthly by Defence Forces Headquarters, Dublin

Collections of:

National Museum of Ireland, Dublin & branch of above at Collins Barracks, Dublin

Army Museum, Collins Barracks, Cork

Army Museum, Curragh Camp, Co. Kildare

Army Museum, Colum Barracks, Mullingar, Co. Westmeath

http://www.irishmilitaryinsignia.com

Cadets from the Military College provide a guard of honour. They wear the current M1961 green service dress, distinguished by the cadet's white/green/white band on the service cap and white shoulder straps. Belts, gloves, and the slings of the Steyr rifles are also white. The left shoulder patch of the college is a yellow and white torch on a rose-pink shield; they also wear a rose-pink lanyard. This will also be the appearance of a new guard-of-honour order of dress for each of the three brigades, differenced by the colours of the central cap band and lanyard. With the introduction of smart service uniforms in the post-war years, the various Corps adopted lanyards in their colours, but the infantry in a great variety of battalion colours rather than their purple Corps colour.

THE PLATES

A: THE 1920s

A1: Corporal, Infantry, 1923
This figure represents a completely equipped soldier, although the task of clothing over 55,000 personnel during the early days of the Civil War was considerable. The green drab cap, tunic and breeches-cut trousers of 1922 are those of the Irish Volunteers, as is the bronze Army crest cap badge (**see detail, bottom right**), set on a green diamond for this rank; and the buttons, which bore a harp between 'I' and 'V' (and continue to do so). The overcoat, which was provided for all ranks, bears the single green cuff stripe of corporal. He wears British 1908 equipment in khaki webbing, and carries the .303in SMLE rifle. Disposable khaki cotton 50-round, five-pocket ammunition clip bandoliers were also common. Brown leather equipment, originally planned and to some extent issued, was impractical for the vastly enlarged army of the Civil War.

A2: General Michael Collins, 1922
This officer was the moving force in organizing the National Army, of which he was the commander-in-chief from its initiation until his death in a Civil War ambush on 22 August 1922. His uniform is of superior quality and a darker, greener shade than that of the rank and file, and is based in most respects on that of the contemporary British Army officer – an exception is the standing collar. The Sam Browne belt with added long holster slings and leg strap was commonly worn by National Army officers. The insignia shown in portraits does not accord with the official regulations which were published later. The blue diamond behind the Army crest on the cap would have been gold/yellow; and the single line of gold 'gimp' on the collar would have been a group of three bars, matching those which Collins already wears on his shoulder straps. In those early days regulations were often flouted. In the midst of the Civil War one of his colleagues complained that another officer was wearing insignia above his station: Collins replied brusquely, 'Oh, let the baby keep his stripes!' As an alternative to the 'overall' trousers with turn-ups, Gen Collins also wore the standard officers' breeches and leggings; this is the order he was wearing during the ambush which caused his death, together with the officers' greatcoat, despite the fact that the action occurred in late August.

A3: Private, Infantry, 1924
The slightly smartened up uniform of the 1924 instructions would remain essentially unchanged until 1938; the cap and tunic were clearly modelled on British Army service dress. The first pattern of Infantry badge, with a central cartouche bearing the battalion number, is worn here. The webbing has been blackened and brought to a high sheen with a mixture of boot polish and candle grease. Arms drill at that period followed the British Army manual, but was changed shortly afterwards to incorporate such movements as the French Army's 'present arms'.

B: THE 1930s

B1: Major, Army Transport Corps, 1930
This is the officer's service uniform worn largely unchanged from 1924 to 1940. The cap and tunic are of green 'whipcord'; breeches of the same changed to pale fawn Bedford cord after 1926. Ankle boots with leggings, laced field boots or these spurred riding boots were worn optionally. The bronze Army crest was displayed on the cap, and bronze rank badges on the sewn-in shoulder straps: here, one bar below two diamonds, all on slightly larger cloth mounts in the lemon-yellow of most non-infantry Corps and Services. On the 2in-high stand collar the silver Corps badges showed a chariot within a riband inscribed 'Diórma Iomchair An Airm'. In 1931 the ATC and elements of the QM General's branch were amalgamated into the Supply & Transport Service (later Corps), and a new collar badge was introduced. The Sam Browne belt supports a brass-hilted sword with a leather knot, in a leather-covered scabbard. Officers of all Corps and Services had worn a dark green lanyard on the left shoulder (or around the neck for senior ranks) to the left breast pocket, but this was discontinued in about 1930.

B2: Sergeant, Artillery Corps, 1936
This immaculate NCO wears the 1924 uniform, but the unit tailor has been persuaded to fit the waist more snugly, and to restyle the breeches with more pronounced 'wings'; their soft leather reinforcement pads are lightened with a creamy 'blanco'. White blanco brightens the Artillery lanyard on his left shoulder; the leggings, boots, and British 1903 bandolier have an almost ruby finish. No doubt the points of his spurs have been cut with a hacksaw and silver threepenny-pieces inserted in the grooves, to give a jaunty 'jingle'. All other items are regulation. The 1928 helmet modelled on the German M1916 has the Army crest mounted on the front, and is entirely blackened. The brass Artillery Corps badges are in a 'handed' pair on the collar, and the red rank bars are worn on both sleeves.

Development of the Infantry Arm/Corps badge. (Left to right) first badge, 1924, with battalion number on cartouche; crude bronze shield format used during the Emergency; first post-war version; current version. The scroll originally bore the word *Ceithernac*, meaning 'Kern', the Irish light footsoldier of the 16th century; the last two badges are inscribed *Cosithe*, also meaning footsoldiers.

1 2 3

4 5 6

7 8 9

10 11 12

13 14 15

16 17 18

INSIGNIA

This shows the basic Corps and Service collar badges in use between 1924 and 1940. There were some changes during and after that period, and others have been modified since 1945, but the essential design elements have remained constant.

(1) Army crest, designed in 1913 for the Irish Volunteers and still the cap badge for all units. 'FF' stands for *'Fianna Fáil'* – the first word is an ancient Gaelic term for an army, the second means 'destiny'.

(2) Infantry Arm and Corps; other examples are illustrated in the photograph opposite.

(3) Artillery Corps – the 'Maid of Erin' seated on a gun above a scroll with a long Gaelic title meaning 'The Group of Heavy Guns'.

(4) Cavalry Corps – the original armoured wheel of the Armoured Car Corps acquired a cuirass, sabre and carbine with the change of title in 1934.

(5) Air Corps

(6) Corps of Engineers – a theodolite in a torque, the ancient Irish gold collar.

(7) Supply & Transport Service, 1931 badge – now entitled Transport & Vehicle Maintenance Corps.

(8) Ordnance Corps – an embossed war shield and a trophy of ancient weapons.

(9) Military Police Corps – entwined 'PA' for *'Poilini an Airm'*.

(10) Signal Corps – now entitled Communications & Information Services Corps.

(11) Army Medical Corps – other ranks' badge in brass. Officers had a completely different badge featuring a silver hand (derived from an Irish legend) flanked by Aesculapius staffs. The Army Medical Service had the distinction of wearing the first official Corps badge in 1923; the AMS soon had specific collar badges for doctors, dentists and pharmacists.

(12) Construction Corps

(13) Department of Defence Administrative Company – this had no commissioned officers.

(14) Military College, 1931 badge – Gaelic motto 'What Deed of Valour Shall I Do Today'.

(15) 1st Division shoulder patch, 1942 – dark blue 'thunderbolt' on orange.

(16) 2nd Division shoulder patch, 1942 – red spearhead on yellow.

(17) School of Music – 1930 badge.

(18) Local Defence Corps, 1940 cap badge – yellow metal and black enamel. Also worn as laper badge on civilian clothing.

B3: Corporal, Cavalry Corps, winter 1939

The original Armoured Car Corps of the Civil War, employing Rolls-Royce, Lancia and Peerless cars, was renamed the Cavalry Corps in 1934. The years of 'the Emergency' would see it at its maximum strength of 80 wheeled AFVs. The most modern were the Landsverk, and Leyland and Dodge cars based upon it. There was also a Carrier Regt with Universal Carriers; in 1943 this was disbanded and the 200-plus carriers were distributed to infantry battalions. On the eve of World War II the Cavalry uniform was virtually unchanged since 1924, though the change of title in 1934 saw the peaked cap exchanged for this headgear, with a black band and swallow-tail ribbons, as being more practical in the confines of a vehicle. The cap was called in the Irish Army a 'glengarry' – confusing to the British, for whom a glengarry is the decorated Scottish sidecap, while the Irish beret is known as a 'caubeen'. The bronze Army crest was worn on the cap, and the Cavalry collar badges (**see detail below**) on both tunic and greatcoat. Here the British 1908 belt and 1903 pistol equipment are worn, all items except the holster being blackened – and note the green lanyard passing across the belt and up to the right shoulder.

C: THE 1930s–40s

C1: Lieutenant, Artillery, Volunteer Force, 1934–40

The Volunteer Force officers' uniform was in the same green whipcord and pale twill cord as the regular officers', but with many detail differences. The headgear was a forage cap, resembling the British field service cap but of taller appearance, with a full height folding false peak and a narrower top gusset. The 2in stand-and-fall collar and pointed cuffs of the tunic were faced with a richer green, as were the detachable shoulder straps. The facings, straps, and front edge were all piped in Corps colour – for the Artillery, orange. Only Artillery orange and Infantry blue seem to have been actually introduced; had the Volunteer Force embraced all the Corps and Services, as planned, a complete colour-coding system for officers' uniforms would have included Air Corps, acid-blue; Cavalry, red; Engineers, brown; Ordnance, magenta; Supply & Transport, violet; Medical, green; Signals, lemon-yellow; and General Service, black. All badges and buttons were chromed metal; this lieutenant wears Artillery collar badges, and conventional shoulder strap bars on orange mounts. All officers wore a dark green lanyard on the right shoulder; and all leather was black.

C2: Volunteer, Infantry, Volunteer Force, 1934–40

The enlisted ranks' uniform was in this greyer shade reminiscent of German field-grey. The chromed Army crest was worn on the left front of the forage cap by all ranks, and Corps badges on the collar. Collar, cuffs and shoulder straps were faced green; for enlisted ranks green piping included the edges of the four pocket flaps. A half-inch green stripe decorated the outseam of the breeches (and two such stripes the officers' green trousers when worn instead of fawn breeches). The black 1928 helmet was issued; the usual 1908 webbing equipment was blackened, including the pack, and the sling of the SMLE rifle. Artillerymen had black leather bandoliers.

C3: Volunteer, Local Defence Force, 1941

Typically, this A Group volunteer wears a blouse and trousers modelled on the 'battledress, denim' of the contemporary British Army (though apparently lacking the large left thigh pocket), in a reddish brown shade; with wear and washing this quickly faded into

a variety of dull browns. The forage cap of the same material bears the LDF cap badge (**see detail below**). His rifle is the .30in US-made P17, usually called a 'Springfield' after the US manufacturer. His only equipment is an American disposable cotton bandolier with six clip pouches.

D: OFFICERS' FULL DRESS, 1935–55

D1: Captain, Infantry

As described in the body text, these blue-black uniforms were differenced for the various Corps and Services with facing colours and gold or silver lace and 'metal'; for Infantry the facing was scarlet and the metal was silver. The sloping-top shako has an upper crown, piping and badge cushion in scarlet, with silver lace, badge and chin cords. The tunic for dismounted branches is single-breasted, piped in facing colour. The collar, piped at top and front in scarlet and at the base in silver, bears Corps badges. Each cuff displays a diagonal band of silver 'shamrock' lace confining a three-point, three-button flap in scarlet. Epaulettes of silver cord bear embroidered gold wire rank badges on scarlet mounts, and a matching lanyard is worn on the left shoulder. (Colonels who held GHQ appointments such as Adjutant General and Quartermaster General wore a more elaborate aiguillette on the right shoulder). The tight overall trousers have a 1½in stripe of scarlet, and are worn over patent leather spurred boots. The sword belt and slings are in red Morocco leather, faced with silver shamrock lace; the buckle with Corps badge is nickel silver; and the sword has a nickel hilt and scabbard and a silver lace knot.

Officers of Cavalry and other mounted branches wore plastron-fronted tunics with two rows of six front buttons; silver rank badges; silver bullion cap lines around the neck, down the back and up around the left shoulder to terminate at the front of the collar; and two ⅝in trouser stripes in facing (scarlet for Cavalry). Cavalry officers wore a patent leather bandolier (pouch belt) with silvered furniture and the Corps badge on the pouch flap. Officers of the Services had a 'crow's foot' – a simple trefoil knot of gold or silver lace above a pointed cuff. White gloves were worn, and white collar and cuffs showed slightly above and below the tunic edges. A version of this uniform was revived in 2003 for the School of Music and military musicians.

D2: Commandant, Signal Corps

The facing is emerald green and the 'metal' gold; note that the cuff lace is horizontal. The quatrefoil design in gold or silver was worn by all officers on the shako crown; the black patent leather peak has the fernleaf embroidery for a field grade officer (generals wore a double row in gold). The cloak is lined with facing-colour artificial silk, and secured with a gilt clasped chain. Belt and slings show gold lace over green leather, and the sword hilt and scabbard are bright brass.

D3: Lieutenant, Air Corps

This Corps' uniform was in a lighter steel-blue, in 'mounted' style with a plastron front;

Rear view of the Volunteer Force enlisted ranks' uniform of the 1930s – see Plate C2. The three-button false pocket flaps on the skirt, and the left edge of the rear vent, are piped green; and note the inverted central pleat above the waist.

facings are scarlet and 'metal' gold, and the cuff flaps are slightly longer and narrower than on the other figures. The collar is edged at top and front with double piping, scarlet outside gold, and at the bottom with gold only; it bears the Air Corps badges (**see detail above, of left side badge**) in a 'handed' pair. The plastrons also have scarlet/gold edging. This pilot wears gold epaulettes and rank badges on scarlet backing, and on his left breast his gilt and enamelled 'wings'. Cavalry-style cap lines are visible around his neck and left shoulder, and his overalls bear Cavalry-style double stripes.

E: THE MOUNTED ESCORT, 1945
E1: Trooper
E2: Lieutenant

When the Artillery Corps was mechanized, a number of horses were retained to serve with a ceremonial escort established in 1931 with the official Gaelic title of 'An Marc Sluagh'; however, they were popularly known as 'The Blue Hussars', reflecting the splendour of the uniforms. The bulk of personnel were drawn from the Artillery Corps, but were not permanently embodied, being called together for rehearsals and public duties as necessary. In addition to ceremonial duties the Blue Hussars performed displays at horse shows and gymkhanas until, with the coming of 'the Emergency', they were disbanded. In 1945 the unit was briefly revived, with some slight alteration to accoutrements (e.g. the disappearance of corner badges from the shabraque), before finally disappearing in 1949 in favour of a Cavalry Corps motorcycle escort (see Plate H3).

The trooper's busby is of black sealskin, with saffron yellow tuft, bag, cap lines and embellishments. The tunic is a rich sapphire blue, with yellow piping and frogging, the breeches white with a yellow stripe, and the riding boots of 'Hessian' pattern. His pouch belt and pouch are of plain black patent leather. A sword with nickel-plated guard and scabbard hangs on white slings from an internal belt; lances were also carried by rankers at displays, but not on escort duties. The officers' uniform was similar, and this rear view shows the same pattern of cording as on other ranks' tunics. The differences are the busby of black sable with a tall feather plume; the pouch of nickel silver, with the gilt Artillery Corps flap badge, on a belt with gold lace facing and gilt furniture; and the fact that all braiding and piping are in yellow silk instead of wool. This lieutenant's shoulder strap rank bars are worked in gold wire embroidery on red mounts.

F: 'THE EMERGENCY', 1939–45
F1: Corporal, 16th Infantry Battalion, c.1942

A slightly lighter green material, christened by the troops 'bull's wool', was used for the M1940 uniform worn by this corporal, with the new forage cap. The tunic has a stand-and-fall collar, bearing the latest version of the Infantry badge, a bronze shield shape. (Later in the war this unit, which served with the independent 5th Bde headquartered at the Curragh, would display the left shoulder patch of Army Troops – a green star on a red shield.) He wears a mixed set of British 1937 webbing: on one side a single 'universal pouch', on the other a brace attachment and a double-pocket 'cartridge carrier'. On parade, he carries the right marker's pennant of the HQ Company of his battalion; the yellow appliqué script and Infantry rifles are sewn to a field

An Artillery sergeant of the Emergency Army, wearing M1940 uniform in green 'bull's wool' fabric. Red rank stripes, brown bandolier and white lanyard are unchanged from the pre-war years, but the brass Corps collar badges have been reduced in size. The badge on his upper right sleeve is not that of a unit but the contemporary Marksman's Badge, of a yellow bow-and-arrow on a red cross.

of that Corps' purple colour. Such flags had no ceremonial significance; they were carried by the right-hand man in the front rank for forming-up purposes. Infantry pennants were triangular and flown on a 6ft 6in ash staff surmounted by a brass finial; the Artillery used a 'burgee' shape, and the Cavalry a swallow-tail format.

F2: Lieutenant, Infantry, 1st Division, 1942

This is the parade order of the officers' service uniform ordered in April 1940, with a notched collar worn open over a shirt collar and tie. Although both the peaked service cap and forage cap were standard for officers of the Emergency Army, on all ceremonial occasions the steel helmet was worn – the British Army's Mk II, painted a light greyish shade. At front centre are painted the badge of 1st Div (**see detail above**) and the white bar identifying 3rd Bde within the division; in cloth, these are also sewn to his left sleeve. His shoulder strap rank bars are still mounted on Infantry purple backing. He wears most of the officers' set from the British 1937 web equipment: belt, braces, pistol holster, binocular case, ammunition and compass pouches – and note the green pistol lanyard. The officers' valise is not attached to the brace ends on the left hip, but may be slung behind. In the field, officers wore the M1940 other ranks' uniform – see page 20.

F3: Gunner, Local Defence Force Artillery, c.1944

From summer 1942 the LDF's denims were replaced with a serge uniform also modelled on British 'battledress, serge': a waist-length blouse, trousers with a left thigh pocket, a beret and greatcoat, together with a gradual issue of 1937 pattern green webbing and steel helmets. (The British-style BD was not issued to the regular Army, who kept the 1940 tunic.) For 'walking-out dress' this gunner has spit-shined his bandolier, gaiters and boots; he still sports the old large Artillery badges on the collar, and has a very long white lanyard on his left shoulder. This was also a period when virtually every self-respecting urban LDF battalion and rural group formed a pipe band, and unit colours were presented.

G: UNITED NATIONS CONTINGENTS, 1960–90

G1: Corporal, 32nd Infantry Battalion; Congo, August 1960

Photos show that the first contingent at Albertville was ill prepared for the climate, and made a motley appearance. The coarse drab green denim blouse and trousers of home fatigue uniform served as makeshift tropical field clothing, with blouse sleeves (and often trouser bottoms) rolled. This NCO is from a photo of a platoon wearing a few of these blue UN caps, but mostly the lightweight plasticized liner from NATO steel helmets modelled on the US M1 (see Plate G2), some peaked service caps, and even 1940 serge tunics. Weapons were the .303in No.4 rifle, Bren LMG, and this Swedish 9mm Carl Gustav M1945 sub-machine gun (note the split-flap 4x magazine pouch); in 1961 the 7.62mm FN self-loading rifle would replace the No.4. Rank chevrons in the 'winged' shape are attached by an elastic loop around his left arm, above a white-on-blue French-language 'ONU' United Nations brassard. The tricolour brassard with blue 'IRELAND' was worn by 32 and 33 Bns in 1960–61. Later photos show the shield insignia (**see detail, centre**) on a khaki left sleeve brassard; this seems to have become standard by 1964. Unit titles were often worn above this, e.g. '38ᵀᴴ INF.BN.' in red on black in April–October 1963. Irish UN unit shoulder titles are

The Mounted Escort trumpeter in 1945, riding a grey; he had a yellow rank stripe on each arm, extensive plaited white aiguillettes from his right to left shoulders, and did not carry a sword (cf Plate E).

a study in themselves; interested readers should visit the website *http://www.irishmilitaryinsignia.com*

G2: Private, 25th Infantry Group; Rabah, Sinai, November 1973

The UN-painted helmet liner is worn, but the steel shell is carried in case of emergency. The high black combat boots, hidden here, appeared in 1961; during the 1960s–70s a range of uniforms were introduced, including this 'working order' of denim-reinforced woollen pullover with a left breast pocket, and a drab green combat uniform with a large map pocket on the left thigh. He carries the FN rifle, and very light belt order still of British 1937 pattern webbing – here, a single pouch and the strapping water bottle carrier, worn on the back of the belt. The UN badge is sewn directly to the pullover's right sleeve, and on the left the national patch (**see detail, centre**). 25th Inf Grp did not wear a unit title; the unit which followed it to the Sinai in April 1974 wore a black-on-red '26 INF GP' title above the Ireland patch.

G3: Company Quartermaster Sergeant, 68th Infantry Battalion; South Lebanon, November 1990

The UN beret is worn with a lightweight drab green short-sleeve shirt (note black-on-green nametag) and slacks; the belt is the fabric type also worn with the green M1961 service tunic. The left brassard (**see detail, left**) bears a white-on-green title '68 IRISH BATT' with 'Gaelic'-shaped Ts, the tricolour national patch adopted in 1988, and the CQMS rank badge. The rank is repeated below the UN patch on a matching right brassard.

From 44 Inf Bn (November 1978–April 1979) to 69 Inf Bn (April–October 1991), all battalions in Lebanon wore titles, in different colours and styles – e.g. black on saffron '48 INF BN' (October 1980–April 1981); and '55 IRISH BATT' in scarlet on green (April–October 1984). From '70 IRISH BATT' (October 1991–April 1992) to '89 IRISH BATT' (April–October 2001), all showed a green arc with yellow lettering and border.

H: HOME SERVICE SINCE 2000

H1: Corporal, 5th Infantry Battalion, Permanent Defence Force, 2002

Combat dress at the beginning of the 21st century has fully caught up with international standards. The black beret is worn by all PDF infantry, bearing the Army crest on a red diamond. The DPM camouflage uniform (in pale grey-green, mid-green, red-brown and black), introduced from 1995 and standard by 2002, is worn here in its winter configuration, over a zipped 'Norwegian' shirt. The hooded parka shows Canadian influence, with expanding pockets, and big buttons for easy handling with gloved hands – note also two different sizes of sleeve pocket, one expanding to take field dressings. Rank is displayed in black on a pale grey-green slide worn on a buttoned chest tab, the name tag on the right chest, and a small tricolour flash on the left shoulder. His harness is the British 1990 pattern Load Carrying Equipment, and his weapon the Austrian 5.56mm Steyr AUG A1 assault rifle, with several plastic components including the clear magazine. His high combat boots, in padded black leather with thick rubber cleated soles, are laced through eyelets on the instep and steel rings on the ankle. Note the slung British GS pattern helmet in its DPM cover.

H2: Private, Reserve Defence Force, 2002
This is essentially a rear view of H1, showing the so-called 'rocket packs' on the back of the drab green equipment. He carries a belt of 7.62mm link for the section's GPMG machine gun. His RDF status is shown by his drab green beret with green badge backing. The 'DPMs' are worn over various other garments depending on climate – thermal vest, T-shirt, pullover (which now also bears the small tricolour left shoulder flash), fleece jacket or Norwegian shirt. From 2001 Naval Service personnel also received a new combat dress very similar to these DPMs but in dark blue; it is worn with a navy-blue beret.

H3: Trooper (3 star), 2nd Cavalry Squadron; Presidential Escort, 2003
Found from the 2nd Cav Sqn, this unit provides a 29-strong Captain's Escort for the President of the Republic and visiting foreign heads of state, and an 18-man Lieutenant's Escort for lesser dignitaries. With his helmet, gauntlets and boots this smart motorcyclist wears the 1961 service tunic, open-collared over a shirt and knit tie, and reinforced cord breeches. The collar bears slanting Cavalry Corps badges; on his left arm is the 2nd Bde patch; and below this a patch of tunic cloth outlined yellow displays the three yellow-edged red stars of his rank. In recent years the use of unit patches on the right shoulder has proliferated; hidden here is that of 2nd Cav Sqn **(see detail, left)**. All officers and NCOs of the Escort are armed; he wears whitened webbing pistol equipment, still of the old British 1937 pattern. Currently, the introduction of a leather jacket for added protection is being considered. The trooper's mount – a 650cc Honda Deauville, painted gloss blue – flies a Cavalry Corps pennon in black, red and green (*erratum* – the green section should be of 'swallow-tail' shape).

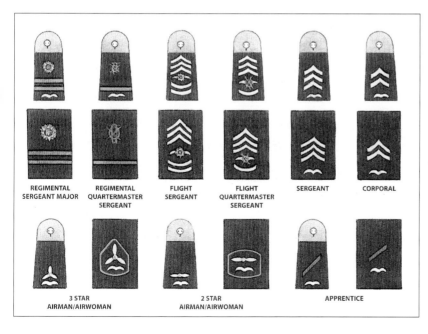

| BRIGADIER GENERAL | COLONEL | LIEUTENANT COLONEL | COMMANDANT |
| CAPTAIN | LIEUTENANT | 2nd LIEUTENANT | CADET |

| REGIMENTAL SERGEANT MAJOR | REGIMENTAL QUARTERMASTER SERGEANT | FLIGHT SERGEANT | FLIGHT QUARTERMASTER SERGEANT | SERGEANT | CORPORAL |
| 3 STAR AIRMAN/AIRWOMAN | | 2 STAR AIRMAN/AIRWOMAN | | APPRENTICE | |

Rank insignia for the Air Corps blue uniform introduced in 1994. Apart from the red shoulder strap bars of RSM and RQMS, all are silver-grey, though with some details – e.g. the super-imposed crests of flight sergeant and flight QM sergeant – in red. Shoulder strap insignia are carried on slides on working dress only, e.g. shirt-sleeve order, pullovers and overalls. All other ranking is worn on the tunic cuffs; it is not worn on overcoats except by the GOC.

INDEX